W9-BCE-617

WITHDRAWN

Scrimshaw

By the same author
Decoupage, A New Look at an Old Craft
Decoupage Designs
The Decoupage Workshop

Scrimshaw

A traditional folk art, A contemporary craft

by Leslie Linsley

photographs by Jon Aron

HAWTHORN BOOKS, INC.
Publishers/New York

SCRIMSHAW

Copyright © 1976 by Leslie Linsley. Copyright under International and Pan-American Copyright Conventions. All rights reserved, including the right to reproduce this book or portions thereof in any form, except for the inclusion of brief quotations in a review. All inquiries should be addressed to Hawthorn Books, Inc., 260 Madison Avenue, New York, New York 10016. This book was manufactured in the United States of America and published simultaneously in Canada by Prentice-Hall of Canada, Limited, 1870 Birchmount Road, Scarborough, Ontario.

Book design by Jon Aron.

Library of Congress Catalog Card Number: 75–28700

ISBN: 0-8015-6608-8

1 2 3 4 5 6 7 8 9 10

Contents

Acknowledgments

After a day of photographing a scrimshander at work, Jon Aron packed up his camera and shook his head, "This can't be work, I'm having too much fun." Working on this book was a rewarding and exciting experience for both of us because the people who contributed their time and work made it so. To them I am grateful, for without them this book would not be the same: Carol Arnold, Robert Spring, Tucker Lindquist, Lesley Zaret, William Haffenreffer, Larry Vienneau, and Richard Peterson. Thanks also to Peter Frey and Linda Anne L'Abbé who are good people, Phil Rose for assuring quality control on all black-and-white prints, and especially to my editor, Joan Nagy, who made it happen.

A basket maker on Nantucket excited the natural instincts of a visiting businessman. "How much would you wholesale those baskets for if I bought in quantity?"

"Same price I quoted you for one," was the reply.

"But I'll buy hundreds and resell them in my store."

"Can't make hundreds. I sell what I make. You got the price."

"But you could make a lot of money. Look, set up an assembly line. Hire a couple of kids, teach 'em how it's done, and you're in business."

The basket maker looked up from his work and asked, "Why?"

Scrimshaw

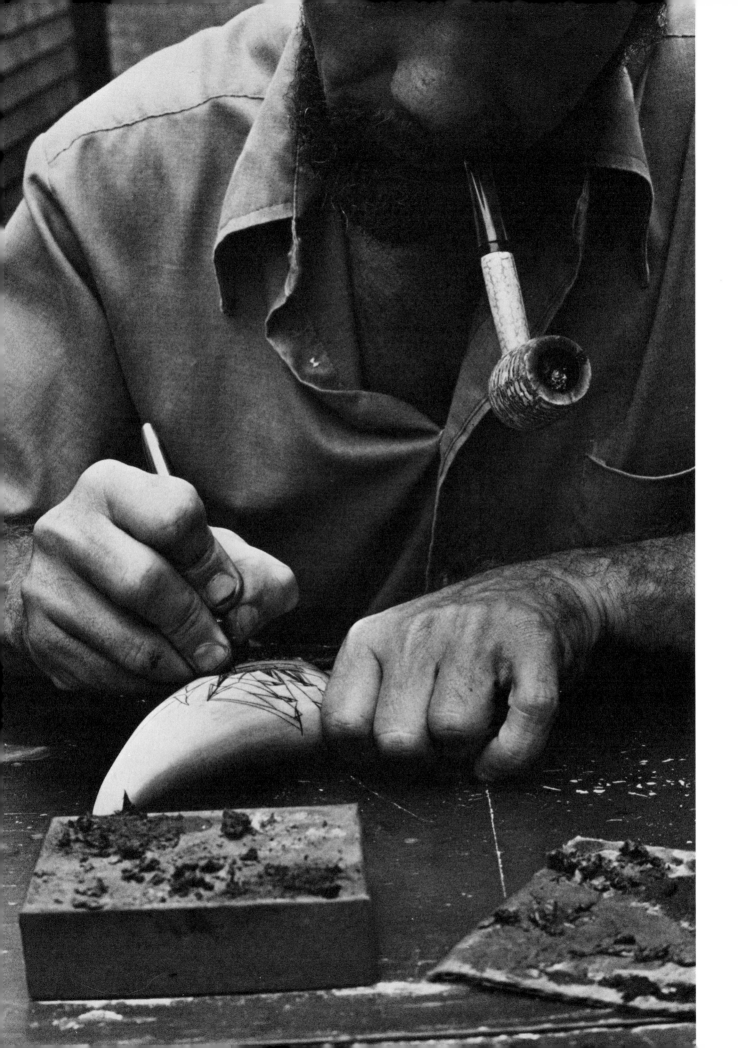

What is scrimshaw?

I don't know exactly when I first became aware of the word *scrimshaw* or even when I first saw the work or knew what it was. Having grown up in sea towns, it seems to me that it has always been a familiar word. It has a pretty sound and most people who hear it for the first time are not sure what it means. When I started to work on this book a friend said, "Is that a place or a person's name?"

Scrimshaw is a craft. It is the scribing of a design on a piece of ivory or bone in order to produce decorative objects, jewelry, and useful items. It is one of the first American folk crafts, originated during the nation's earliest years by New England whalers who spent several years at sea. To relieve the boredom, these sailors spent their leisure time drawing and scribing on whale's teeth and whalebone. The scenes that were scribed depicted the activities and dreams that took place during their long voyages. These items have become the most sought after collectibles of Americana. Today's scrimshanders practice the craft as it was originated in New England and also develop innovations in subject and material that are not restricted to the nautical theme.

The technique of scrimshaw is not difficult to learn and many crafters and artists are using this technique to express their creativity in a new form.

Quite simply the process goes like this. The material you are working on is sanded until smooth. It can be a piece of ivory, shell, bone, or even plastic. It is then polished and that is all the preparation needed. Some crafters eliminate the polishing, but this is an added dimension that is preferred by most.

Then the design is drawn onto the surface with a pencil. If the crafter cannot draw well, a design can be traced and transferred onto the object. Now you are ready to scribe each pencilled line with a sharp tool, such as an X-Acto knife blade, an Intaglio point, or any other sharp pointed instrument, such as a dentist's tool.

Once the lines are incised you will fill them in by applying ink, dyes, or oil paint to the surface and wiping it away. The areas that were incised will be filled in with color. As you get more

This purse is made completely of whalebone and scrimshawed by Carol Arnold with her distinctive wildflower designs.

experienced with the tools you will be able to create more and more interesting designs.

In the beginning it is a good idea to stick to very simple designs until you have become familiar with the technique. As with any new skill, if you rush in and begin over your head, the project will never get finished and you will become quickly discouraged. If you do a simple project while learning, you will be eager to try again.

The technique of scrimshaw can be easily learned. Once you know how to do it, you can create almost any kind of design. There are many contemporary artists and crafters who are creating some of the most exciting pieces of scrimshaw ever done. Their work is valued as fine art just as the scrimshaw of ninteenth century sailors is valued for its historic significance.

When learning a new craft it is always best to see the work of those people who are considered to be exceptional in their area. In this way we can be encouraged and influenced so that we have something to strive for. Often someone else's work may spark an idea for something original.

In the beginning it is often good to copy a design until the crafting technique becomes familiar. Learning the process is the beginning and this can offer real joy. However, the most exciting part of learning a new craft is creating your own designs. For some reason it seems to be difficult to convince people that this is true. It is so satisfying to create an original piece even if it is a very simple design. As you practice, your style will become more definite. Often designs are copied, so even if you can't draw at all, you can trace or copy subjects from books. Making the decision and putting together a design often challenges your creative instincts. Soon you will be creating your own designs.

Nautical scenes were used most often because this was what the original scrimshanders saw all day. Today, scrimshaw is mostly done in sea towns and nautical themes are still the most popular. In Nantucket, Massachusetts, for instance, seagulls, the Old Mill, wildflowers, as well as ships, are commonly used for scrimshaw themes since the natural influence is hard to ignore.

Scrimshaw is one of the few crafts with a romantic history. Imagine signing onto a whaling vessel for a three- or four-year voyage. Most of the whalers were inexperienced, coming from small towns and farms and seeking the romance of the sea. There were often long, boring periods between the capturing and processing of whales, and once all chores were done there was lots of time to spare.

Sperm whales were pursued all over the world for their superior oil; the fact that these whales have teeth was of added interest. Each sailor was allotted his share of teeth or bone (the teeth were divided up according to rank and then the trading began) to decorate or carve as he wished, and this became a very pleasant way to pass the long hours. Some reports have it that the men became so involved with their scrimshandering that they would often pretend not to spot a whale so that they could continue this enjoyable endeavor known as "the idle" or "lazy man's" activity.

Some of the items that were carved and scrimshawed in those early whaling days were ornamental objects, ingenious toys, useful items to bring back to wives, as well as equipment to be used on the ship.

Sewing boxes were favorite items and were usually scribed with details of the life at sea as well as fanciful scenes. Writing desks, clothes pins, rolling pins, jewelry, combs, pie crimpers, ditty boxes, and stamps for log books are some of the varied objects found in museums today. It is exciting to see that period in our country's history visually recorded on the scrimshawed items that have been carefully collected and preserved.

To scribe on the ivory or bone whalers used tools that were readily on hand: jackknife, sail needle embedded in a wooden handle, or even a finely sharpened nail. Most early scrimshaw was colored with black ink or soot. However, occasionally color was added from tobacco juice, the juice of berries, and other plants from tropical South Sea islands often visited by the sailors.

Among the sailors, there were many fine draftsmen, but since most of the early scrimshanders were not artists, they either produced fairly crude drawings or traced designs from magazines of the day. Before the long voyage, the sailors' wives would place books and magazines aboard ship. It was from these early Godey magazines that the whalers copied fanciful scenes and pictures of women on the whale's teeth.

Today's scrimshander is still doing pretty much what the old scrimshander did, only better. Because there is no more whaling done in this country, the availability of whale's teeth is limited to what is left from several years ago when supplies were imported from other countries. But importation is no longer legal. Scrimshanders are turning to substitute materials, such as elephant and walrus ivory, antlers, cow and beef bone, shell, vegetable ivory, and plastic.

Scrimshaw as a new craft hobby has everything going for it. Anybody, any age or sex, is able to do it. It can be done almost anywhere—a corner of a room provides enough space. The tools are simple to use and obtain. No formal training is needed, although a bit of drawing knowledge is helpful. Finally, a simple project can be completed in a few hours.

Summary of process

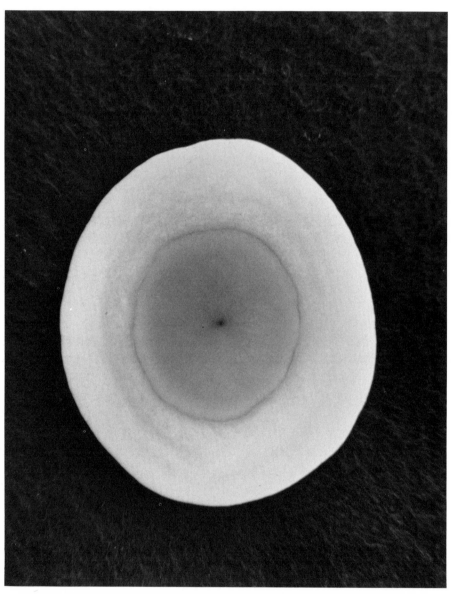

Scrimshaw is the craft of scribing on ivory and filling in the incised lines with color to form a design. Begin with a blank disc and prepare it by sanding until smooth. If the sandpaper is slightly wet, the surface will eventually feel like satin. Other materials for scrimshaw projects are shell, bone, plastic, antlers, and ivory nuts.

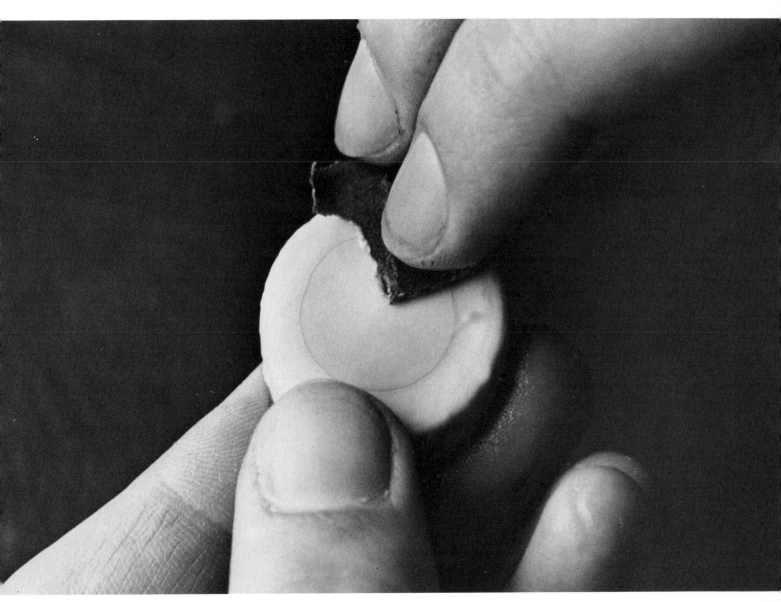

A piece of black, wet or dry sandpaper is slightly dampened for a final sanding to polish the ivory. If you are working on material other than ivory, such as a shell, you can give it a once-over with the fine sandpaper. Plastic does not need to be sanded.

Choose a design that you like. It can be inspired from a book of illustrations. If you are fairly good at drawing, make up your own design. If not, a design can be traced from a book and transferred. Keep the first project simple while learning the technique. Draw the design on the disc with a pencil.

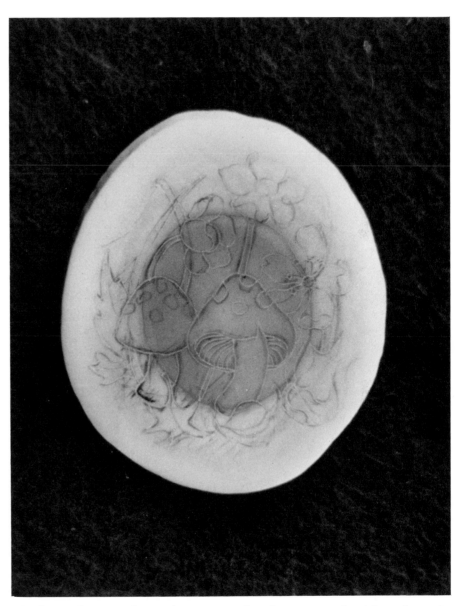

The lines that you have drawn can then be engraved with a sharp instrument such as an X-Acto knife, an old dentist tool, a penknife, an intaglio point, a sharp nail embedded in a handle, or a sail needle. Carefully apply pressure to the instrument in order to penetrate the surface of the material.

Using india ink, oil paint, or watercolor dyes, paint over the areas that you have incised. You can use a small pointed artist's brush to do this. If you want the design to be multicolored, scribe each part, fill it with color, then scribe the next part to be filled in with another color.

With a clean cloth, wipe away the ink or paint. Your scribed lines will be filled in and the excess will be cleaned off the surface, revealing your design. You may simply want to outline the design in black before engraving the detailed lines to be filled in with different colors.

Add more engraved lines in areas where you will want a concentration of color. If you engrave the lines close together, the color will appear darker. Do not paint on the surface. The color should only appear in the engraved lines.

The more you scribe, the more detail you can add. Try not to let the colors overlap. This scrimshawed necklace by Carol Arnold is done in red, pink, purple, brown, and green. Using a small drill, such as a Dremel motor tool, make a small hole in the top of the disc. Bend a piece of wire and insert. A chain of the desired length is then added to complete the project.

Piano keys make excellent earrings or can be strung together on a chain for a necklace. Carol Arnold used her version of a nautical theme on this pair.

What to make

Before you begin doing scrimshaw, you will want to decide what to make. Ivory is so clean and sensuous looking that it is excellent for decorative objects and jewelry. Slabs of ivory cut from tusks can be made into small boxes or used for belt buckles. Shells can be made into jewelery and are excellent for a first project. Old ivory piano keys, once scrimshawed, make lovely earrings, or several can be arranged on a chain for an interesting necklace. The famous Nantucket lightship baskets are topped with a scrimshawed ivory oval. Some have intricate whaling scenes, others are adorned with whimsical flowers and mushrooms. Recently at a tag sale I saw a set of six mother-of-pearl–handled knives for four dollars. These would have been an excellent scrimshaw project.

All the substitutes for ivory listed on pages 19–21 can be used to make any scrimshaw projects. For instance, deer antlers make fine rings and cow bone makes interesting napkin rings. Like beef bone, they also can be used for decorative objects. To cut a tusk, antler, cow bone, or tooth, use a hacksaw. Mark off your cutting lines, hold the object in a vise and cut.

Ivory nuts are small meaty nuts that become extremely hard when baked in an oven. They are a bit darker in color than real ivory and are often used to make rings, buttons, key chain decorations and other small items including earrings, tie tacks, and cuff links. This is a beautiful natural material and easy to work with.

This little basket holds the ivory discs that were cut for Carol's work. Holding a tooth in a vise, the discs are first marked with a pencil and then sliced with a hacksaw. The narrow end produces smaller discs and the middle section provides a disc that can be used as a belt buckle.

Materials to scrimshaw

Whale's teeth and elephant ivory are the materials most commonly used for scrimshaw. The surface is just right for scribing, not as brittle or hard as bone. Craft shops and gift shops located in sea towns often have a supply which was bought before the moratorium on whales and before it was illegal to transport whale products into this country.

Although ivory is becoming scarce in this country, there are still odds and ends of old ivory pieces to be found. Since I am an inveterate collector of junk, I can usually be found in thrift shops, antique stores, and local dumps. Don't overlook these places as a possible source for materials to scrimshaw. This can be an interesting and fun way to begin your new hobby.

Vegetable ivory has been used as a substitute for ivory since the middle of the nineteenth century, but scrimshanders are just

These ivory nuts are from the ivory palm tree. The small white piece in the center is the inside of the brown nuts. When baked, these ivory nuts become hard and resemble real ivory in texture and color and are used frequently as an ivory substitute.

Deer antlers are an excellent substitute material for ivory. Often found shed in the woods, they can be cut, sanded, and polished for rings, small jewelry pieces, as well as decorative items. The surface is quite good for scribing.

beginning to explore its possibilities. The source of the ivory nut is the ivory palm tree that grows in South America. The nuts grow in clusters. Each nut resembles a Brazil nut; it is brown and rough skinned. Inside is a hard center which looks and feels exactly like ivory in texture and color. This is referred to as the ivory nut. Sometimes, if soft, it is necessary to bake the ivory nut for a few minutes in an oven (preheated to 300°) to ensure hardness for scribing.

The ivory nuts are sold in bulk and a minimum order is ten pounds at approximately three dollars a pound. The nuts, polishing compound, and other material for doing scrimshaw are available through the mail. (See page 162)

Old ivory piano keys are great for scrimshaw. But todays new plastic ones have just as much potential. You can purchase a set of fifty-two ivory-colored, plastic keys for approximately fifteen dollars. (See page 163)

Deer antlers are grey in color and can be sanded so that they are smooth and whiter in color than ivory. The piece on the right hasn't been sanded. The other piece has been sanded smooth.

Other materials that can be scrimshawed include cow bone and cow horns, both an excellent substitute for whale's teeth. Shed deer antlers are often found in the woods. While the antlers are grey in color rather than an off-white like the ivory, the material is quite good to work on. Another natural material is shell. And you can't beat the price! Most shells have been naturally polished by the sand and waves and can be scrimshawed without any preparation.

Wood is another possibility, but it should be sanded if not already smooth. I found when experimenting that if a wooden box is painted white and several coats of polyurethane varnish are applied, the color changes to ivory, and the surface will be hard enough to scrimshaw carefully. Wooden boxes can be purchased in hobby shops or you might find an old, interesting one in your attic or at the thrift shop.

Scrimshanders are already using beef bone for work that is sold across state lines (see Scrimshaw Art Preservation Act, pages 134–135). First the bone is boiled to remove all the meat and as much of the bone marrow as possible. This creates a terrible odor, but if you drop a clove into the water, it will take away some of the smell. Next, the bone should dry for a couple of days, preferably in the sun. Once sanded and polished, it is amazing how clean and white an ordinary soup bone can be made to look.

Sanding and polishing

If you will be working on a material that has a rough surface such as a whale's tooth, elephant ivory, beef bone, cow horn, or deer antlers, you will begin by sanding and polishing.

To sand by hand, you will need three grades of sandpaper: 3M Wet or Dry in medium #220 and very fine grits of #400 and #600. Sanding by hand is an interesting experience. It has a calming effect, and it is quite pleasant to sit back with your piece of ivory and sandpaper in hand and let your thoughts wander as you rhythmically sand away. A sailing friend of mine took up the craft because he felt it was a shame to waste the opportunity to fantasize himself as an old whaler. "When out there in the middle of the ocean, I just lean back with my scrimshaw in hand and daydream. I can almost make myself believe that I'm on a whaling ship two hundred years ago," he told me.

Most present-day crafters use an electric hand sander. This is an electric drill with a sanding disc attachment. A quick spin over the surface will remove all rough areas. When working on a tooth or horn this should be done quickly before the material gets too hot. If too much heat builds up, the material will crack. You can avoid this by sanding by hand. This takes a while longer but it is easier to control the buildup of heat.

Sanding should be done outside or in a well-ventilated room. The ivory dust builds up in the air and is quite smelly and harmful when breathed into the lungs. One crafter I know wears a surgical mask.

Once the material is sanded it can be polished. The polishing compound looks like a cake of yellow soap and is called by several different names. Some call it tripoli, others call it bobbing compound. By whatever name, it is essentially a jeweler's polishing material, and you can try a local jeweler for some, or, if unsuccessful, a wholesale jewelry supply house. Apply this with a clean cloth and buff like mad. A soft mellow sheen will appear.

Instead of the polishing compound, you can use a very fine #0000 steel wool for the final smoothing of the material. There are often scratches formed by the sand that are not immediately visible and this final polishing eliminates them.

A disc is polished with a jeweler's buffing wheel. A polishing compound is first rubbed onto the soft material of the wheel. If you have long hair be sure to keep it out of your way so that it won't get caught if you will be working with something similar to the buffing wheel.

As with ivory, bone is sanded with #220 sandpaper, a second sanding with #400 and finished with #600 for the last touch. Before hand sanding, an electric sander can be used for a quick once-over to be sure that all splintered pieces of bone are removed as well as any particles that did not come off in the boiling process. When sanding the bone with #400, wet the sandpaper slightly for extra smoothness. The bone is then polished with the polishing compound.

Larry Vienneau does a rough sketch of a nautical scene on an old whale's tooth that he has been commissioned to scrimshaw. He suggests that you plan out the entire scene before beginning. The details are then added as he scribes.

Choosing a design

Creating your own designs is the most exciting and challenging part of learning a new craft. If you are unable to draw, choosing a design can be as satisfying. Keep the design simple in the beginning.

"Where can I look for design inspiration?" you might ask. Inspiration for designs can be found everywhere. Illustrated books are an excellent source for ideas. Dover Press, for example, has published many paperback design books that can be found in bookstores, if not your local library. One book contains only art deco designs, which are excellent for simple patterns. A book of American Indian designs offers another form of inspiration. Another book contains geometric symbols. Typographic books are excellent for tracing or adapting lettering. Books of old engravings offer yet another area for subject ideas. Folk art designs are exciting and varied and can be easily adapted for a simple scrimshaw project.

Many art books can be used for reference. Look at the illustrations to see how lines are actually drawn. It might be worthwhile to look at books on pen and ink drawings, both how-to-do-it books as well as books by famous artists. In addition, fine pen and ink drawings by political satirists and illustrators can be seen in magazines and newspapers. Notice how they shade, the quality of their line, and what they leave out. All of these things will give you an understanding of the basic techniques of scrimshaw. (See the list of suggested reference books in the appendix.)

Books on wildflowers are interesting to study. Some flowers are more intricately drawn than others and contain more detail. Look for details. Do not simply look at the overall effect.

Often we look at things without really seeing them. When you are concerned with every line of a petal you will look at an illustration with the understanding that you will be drawing and scribing each separate line. Everything is looked at microscopically. This is quite different from painting a picture. Scrimshaw cannot be loose; at its best it is precise. Each line is an important part of the whole. Since you will generally be working on a small area the designs will be rather small and scaled down.

Pendant by Carol Arnold

You therefore have the opportunity to concentrate, for instance, on a tiny flower until you feel you have it right.

A simple flower design is the easiest to scrimshaw because the lines are loose and can be a bit more unplanned and less rigid than a ship, for instance. A flower can be as intricate as you want to make it depending on how many scribed lines you use. The more detail you draw and scribe, the more elaborate your scrimshaw becomes. In other words, if you are working on the petal of a flower, and scratch a few lines inside the petal outline, when you apply your ink or paint, it will fill in the scribed lines. The more lines you scratch onto the tiny petal, the more detailed and professional your scrimshaw will appear.

When first learning to do a craft it is sometimes best to study the designs of accomplished artists. If you are attracted to the nautical theme, take a look at the photographs of Robert Spring's and Larry Vienneau's work. If you have the opportunity you might enjoy a visit to a whaling museum where you can see fine examples of scrimshaw from the past.

When choosing a design, it is good to take a careful look at the object you will be working on. Often the design in a book seems smaller than it is because of its relation to the page, but when copied onto a small ivory disc it may be overpowering.

This decorative whale's tooth is done by Robert Spring and mounted on a wooden stand. It is an excellent example of the fine craftsmanship being done by our modern-day scrimshanders.

Perhaps you prefer a fanciful dragon, or a simple butterfly. An initial on a pendant is fun to try, but you should first practice making letters. Take the time to look at books. The more you see, the more ideas you will get. Greeting paper and cards can be another source of design inspiration. Often an illustration is a reference for part of a design that can be combined with something you create. For instance, you may want to trace the outline of a ship and add a decorative border to the outer rim of your piece. This border might be one you draw yourself or a design that could be adapted from something you have seen.

Another idea might be simple Oriental designs. If you can find a bird book with small illustrations, you may be able to use this as a design source.

Geometric designs are often best left until you have perfected your scribing skills. Scribing several strokes over and over in an identical fashion is often more difficult than it looks. Trees with winding branches are fun to scrimshaw, and because of the carefree nature of the subject mistakes can be covered up or diverted. Animals are harder to scribe, especially if you are working on a facial expression. They are a difficult challenge to draw, let alone scribe.

Mushrooms make an interesting first subject because there are large areas to work on. You can shade them, using the crosshatch method, or outline them the way Carol Arnold does. They can be realistic or fanciful and therefore a good practice subject.

Most of the craftspeople that I talked to agreed that the easiest design for a beginner is one that is rather large, and not too detailed. A whale, for instance, or another object with a solid area, eliminates the concern of where to place the scribed lines and can be done with a bit less control. This will allow you the opportunity to familiarize yourself with the technique. You will learn how to hold the scriber in order to make straight and curved lines. Of course the most important thing to remember when choosing a design is to choose one that you like. If you don't care for the subject you will not be enthusiastic and will probably turn off to this craft before you turn on to it.

Transferring and scribing the design

If you don't feel confident drawing a design freehand, try tracing a design from a book and transferring it to the surface you are working on. Be sure that it is a suitable size or you will have to scale it down.

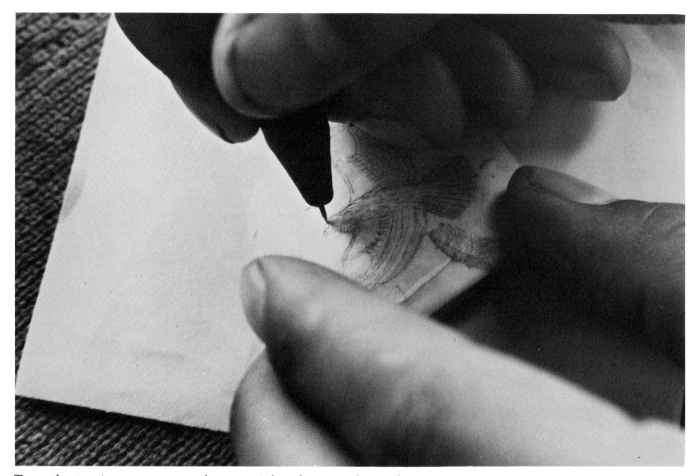

Tape the tracing paper onto the material and, using the scriber, press through the paper making small pinholes through the entire outline.

Very few professional scrimshanders scribe a design without first drawing it on the piece they plan to scrimshaw. If you are artistically talented, sketch your design directly onto the surface with a sharp pencil. If you don't feel that you are able to draw well enough, you can trace and transfer a design from a book or greeting card or similar source.

If the design is too large (or too small), the grid method provides an easy solution. Using ruler and pencil, divide your design into equal squares, like a checkerboard. Next determine the size of the area you want the design to cover. Make one large square that size and divide it into the same number of squares that you used to divide the design. Now you are ready to reduce or enlarge your original. Transfer the design one square at a time, matching square for square. After all the squares are filled in you will have a replica of the design that's ready to be transferred.

Using a pencil and a piece of tracing paper, trace your design. Now tape the tracing in place on the object to be scrimshawed. With the scribe, make dots right through the tracing paper onto the surface. The dots should be close enough together to clearly

Remove the tracing and join the dots with the scriber. Fill in with ink.
Now you can go on adding details the same way.

delineate the outline of the design when the tracing paper is removed. Details can be added in this same way. Remove the tracing and ink the surface of the piece. Remove the ink with a clean cloth and the dotted outline of the design will remain. With your carving tool connect the dots. Ink the lines and wipe again. You should have a complete outline of the design.

Years ago when whalers first did scrimshaw they used the tools that were familiar to them. Today we have better materials available and don't have to be limited to those often-awkward tools. An incisor, dental tools, an X-Acto knife, or intaglio points are perfect. X-Acto knives with different size blades are available in art supply stores, as are intaglio points (a package of ten intaglio points sells for about a dollar). You can probably find an old dentist tool or other sharp instrument by poking around thrift shops or asking your dentist. You might find a sharp instrument in your kitchen drawer. As a matter of fact, any sharp pointed instrument that you feel comfortable with can be used. Some people have even tried using a push pin or a record needle that has been secured to a wooden dowel.

To make a simple, inexpensive tool get some intaglio points or nails and make or buy a few dowels in a hardware store. Clamp the dowel in a vise and pound the intaglio point into one end of the dowel then sharpen the exposed point. If using a nail, file off the head and sharpen the end on a sharpening stone so that both ends are pointed. Insert one end in the dowel and use the other to scribe.

Many scrimshanders have several scribing tools to engrave lines of varying thicknesses. It is important to keep these tools sharpened.

Once your design is drawn onto the surface of your object, you will begin the scribing. If you have transferred your design, you will fill in the areas with various incised lines. When you first make the scratches they are difficult to see and you really need strong light on your piece to perceive the marks. A small intensity light is good for this purpose.

Some of the details can be curved lines, others straight for shaded areas. The entire design should not be filled in. Hold your scriber very tightly and press down hard in order to penetrate the surface you are working on. Shell and bone are quite brittle. As you work, the excess material that is being scratched away will build up slightly on either side of your incised lines. This is just a bit of dust, but it should be blown away before adding the ink, because the dust will absorb the color and make the lines very fuzzy. Try to achieve a nice, clean, sure-looking line that does not appear choppy.

If you are working on a flower, let the lines be close together and follow the curve of each petal. Straight lines can be made for the stem. Curved lines should be used for the leaves. The more lines that you scribe close together, the more intense the color will appear. If the lines are thin, the color will be faint; thicker lines will make the color appear darker. For instance, the center curved line of a leaf may be a bit thicker and will create a heavier look. The curved lines on either side of the main vein can be very thin, close lines and they will look more delicate. Different tools will vary the effect. Robert Spring has an easy and interesting lesson on pages 69–71 to help you learn technique.

Ink and rub

Once the design is scribed the lines are barely perceptible. Ink, paint, or dye is rubbed over the surface and then wiped away leaving the color in the carved lines only. Do not paint on the surface, merely leaving it to dry. This is not scrimshaw and the color will wear away or rub off. This is one of the ways to recognize well-crafted, professional scrimshaw. Color is created by filling the scribed lines, and if more color is needed in different areas, add more lines and then more color.

Today, many scrimshanders who are influenced by the original scrimshanders' work use black india ink exclusively. But oil paint in black, raw umber, and burnt sienna also creates an interesting effect. When using oil paint, squirt it onto a corrugated paper so that some of the excess oil is absorbed. The paint can be applied with a brush or finger. Rub it into the design area that you are working on. Rub off the excess, leaving your newly scribed design filled in. This is as exciting an experience the first time as I expect it is after the hundredth.

When you apply the color it is a real thrill to see your design appear almost by magic. For better or worse, there it is. If you don't like what you see, however, it is not the end of your scrimshaw career. Just sand it off and start again. You can remove the design as long as you haven't made a deeply etched error that is in a hard to get at spot. The detail of a small flower that has already been scrimshawed with many crisscrossing lines could be difficult to remove. A detail on a ship that goes wrong is not easy for the amateur to remove. You either live with it or begin from the beginning. I know, I know! I couldn't do it the first time either.

Watercolor dyes can be used in place of oil paint, and they come in a variety of colors. Dr. Martin or Pelikan are two brands that are often used. These must be applied with a very narrow pointed artist's brush. Just dip it in the color, wipe off some of the excess by brushing it on a scrap of paper, and then apply the paint to the area.

When using several colors, it may be easier to scribe just the area that will be one color. Apply the ink and wipe it off before going onto the next area. When applying different colors to lines that are close to one another, you have to be careful so that one color doesn't seep over into the other. If, for instance, you have created petals that will be pink and you have a center that will be green, you have to apply the green so that it won't run into the petals. Take special care when rubbing off the excess. If the green does overlap onto the pink, simply re-apply the pink. If the ink dries, use a little water on your cloth to rub it off. Continue to scribe and ink until the design is completely filled in. If it needs more detail or more color, this can be done when you are finished inking. If you want heavier color in certain areas, this is done by adding more carved lines and filling in with more color.

Every crafter seems to have a favorite material: an old scriber, a worn-out cloth. Almost everyone that I met had a different special something to rest their work on. Most of the materials were beat up with age and use. A terry cloth towel worked well for one scrimshander who had been using it to wipe away paint from every scrimshaw piece he'd ever made. Scrap pieces of leather were used to cover a work surface to rest ivory upon so that it wouldn't scratch. Plain old tissue paper and Kleenex were used for wiping off or absorbing excess ink when necessary.

When wiping away the paint or ink it should not be done expansively. You should wipe away the tiny area as close to the filled-in lines as possible to avoid staining the rest of the piece with the color you are using.

If you are making a necklace, drill a small hole in the top of your piece with a drill, such as a Dremel motor tool. With a jeweler's pliers or similar handy object, twist a piece of wire into a small loop. Cut off any excess with a wire cutter leaving a small post to insert into the drilled hole. Before inserting the post, put a drop of epoxy glue in the hole. Once the post is inserted, set the piece aside to dry. A silver or gold chain can be purchased to run through the loop. If you have made earrings, drill small holes through the top of the scrimshaw and add your earring findings. These jewelry findings are available in hobby and craft shops or from a jewelry supply house.

And that is all there is to it. The process that is. The creative potential, however, is enormous.

Dick Peterson's birds in flight are a familiar scene from his studio window. He uses a navy blue, almost black, watercolor ink for this scrimshawed piece.

Preserving scrimshaw

Some scrimshanders use linseed oil to preserve scrimshaw made of ivory; others leave it as is. Since the natural moisture is boiled out of whale's teeth, it sometimes has a tendency to dry out and crack. It is wise, therefore, to apply a coat of linseed oil to such a piece about twice a year. Some of the boiled-out oil must be replaced.

Never leave a piece of ivory in the direct sun or near a radiator for any length of time. Some museums keep a container of water inside a closed case of scrimshaw to preserve the pieces and prevent them from drying out. Even the heat from your body will cause a ring to crack after a long period of time if not treated properly. Perfume, for some reason, also causes cracking.

If you go swimming with a scrimshaw necklace around your neck, the salt water or chlorine will fade the color. To preserve the scrimshaw's color do not expose it to salt water, chlorine, or direct sunlight.

The Nantucket lightship basket originated a hundred years ago when lonely lighthouse keepers passed the long hours making baskets which were later decorated with ivory carvings. The original wooden molds are still used for these purses today, and the men and women who make them on Nantucket are backed up with orders for two and three years. This cane basket was made by William Sayle and scrimshawed by Robert Spring with the steamer Nantucket.

The scrimshander

As with any other craft, scrimshaw is an intimate experience and a personal expression. The end result is determined by what the individual brings to the craft: knowledge of the technique and materials, the inborn talent, the experience at working at the craft, and experiences as a person. The history of scrimshaw is interesting, and it is fascinating to view the finished work of fine scrimshanders. However, it is the person doing the craft, that moment of the hands coming together with the tools and materials, that makes the craft come alive and have meaning. We can watch the piece being made, but we cannot watch the creative process. This takes place within the person doing the craft, and all we can see are the end results. The obvious thing about scrimshaw as a craft is that the materials and technique are simple and direct. There are few hidden secrets, and the people doing the craft are open and genuinely willing to share their individual techniques and "tricks of the trade."

Each crafter works differently and approaches his or her work in an individual way. Sometimes the doing is more important than the finished work. That is, the developing of a handcrafted item is a very satisfying experience, and the challenge of learning new ways to do it better is quite rewarding. The finished item represents the end of that experience until it begins again.

No matter what the craft is, the crafter solves individual problems while working, often by trial and error. He or she is constantly involved with the craft and able to share particular ideas that would be helpful for the beginner. This is not to say that each scrimshander is giving away a guarded secret. Since it is the combined experiences of each person that makes his or her work unique, this cannot be given away, only shared. If two people learn to do scrimshaw together, the work that they each do would not look exactly alike. The technique of a craft can be learned, new ways to improve the skills can be shared, but the finished piece is an individual expression. This is what sets one craft designer's work off from another's. Design and technique are interrelated.

As a designer, I feel an understanding of the crafter's

relationship to the work and the environment. The crafting experience is an individual one. It is often peaceful, sometimes frustrating, most times exhilarating. But it is *always* a personal one. There is nothing to replace the opportunity of being right there and watching the person in his or her workshop in order to learn a craft. It was therefore with special appreciation that I shared this experience through knowing the people who allowed me to come into their workshops in order to present their work to you.

There are many fine scrimshanders in the United States. Many of them live in seaport towns like New Bedford and Nantucket, Massachusetts. Having been the centers of the whaling industry, the influences of this part of our history are strongly felt in these communities.

I have chosen to present the work of scrimshanders on Nantucket Island for several reasons. Partially because it is a romantic and nostalgic setting for scrimshaw, but mostly because there is a great deal of activity being done here in terms of fine and varied craftwork. This in no way reflects on the other fine scrimshanders whose work is not shown. The work selected represents different aspects of the craft, each in the crafter's individual style.

All the scrimshanders whose work I have presented were living on Nantucket at the time of the writing of this book. Nantucket is a tiny island thirty miles off the coast of Massachusetts. Whaling was the main source of Nantucket's income and in 1843, Nantucket harbored eighty-eight ships. The last Nantucket whaling vessel sailed in 1868. A visit to Nantucket is like stepping back into the eighteenth and nineteenth centuries. The beautiful homes of the great whaling captains are still maintained by the Nantucket Historical Association. The Whaling Museum houses some of the finest and oldest scrimshaw, as well as examples of many ivory carvings. There are books and records about scrimshaw and the early whaling days. The library in the museum also offers books and information on the preservation of endangered species.

Carol Arnold

At the beginning of the summer, I began to notice many girls wearing delightful scrimshawed necklaces. The ivory discs were covered with gay wildflowers, mushrooms, and tiny bugs. Others were designed with symmetrical and geometric patterns. A crazy dragon adorned another, and sometimes a nude lady would be the theme. All of these pieces were done in a similar style. They had a contemporary feeling, were well designed, well drawn, and very colorful. Definitely not a copy from past scrimshaw.

Whenever I stopped to ask who had done the piece, each time the answer was the same, Carol Arnold. When Jon and I met Carol we liked her instantly, and her work was a delight to photograph. Being relatively new to the craft, she is quite open to learning and improving her technique. Every time I saw her she had discovered something new that she was trying.

As an art school graduate, Carol is quite adept at drawing and designing. When she's drawing flowers she looks at the actual flower to see how it is formed. Usually she'll pick blades of grass until she finds the one that she likes for her design. Often she uses illustrated books for reference. After all, if you're drawing a lion it's a bit difficult to find just the right lion in your backyard. Although design ideas are inspired by books, Carol adapts a bit here and there to create her own style.

This is what sets one person's scrimshaw apart from another's. Some crafters become more skillful with the technique, but a

really well-done piece must combine good design or rendering with good technique.

Crafting skill alone is not enough to create an excellent piece. Design is as important and often this is not understood by the casual observer. It is this imaginative creative input from the designer that sets his or her work apart from another's. All your cross-hatching may be perfect, but if the border isn't well designed, the scrimshaw is not as well done as it could be. It is this combination of crafter and designer that is evident in Carol's work. When she is alone in her studio with her scribe and ivory in hand, her interpretations of what she perceives and feels are reflected in her designs.

Carol combines her talents with those of Dennis Higgins, a metal smith and jewelry designer. Dennis and Carol are imaginative and innovative in their approach to their crafts. Once when Dennis was making ivory boxes, I got very excited about their originality and exquisite work. Dennis claimed that he was simply making more things for Carol to scrimshaw, but this is far from the truth. His delicate silver and gold work is as unusual as Carol's scrimshaw designs. One thing that Dennis said to us that has stuck with me was, "The world is cluttered with junk, some of it is called art. I don't want to contribute more junk to the world. I want to create something beautiful."

Sometimes they work separately, and when they do, Dennis takes off in a whole new direction planning future projects. The most recent "invention" was finished just before we left. Right now industry is being carefully analyzed regarding toxic chemicals and other pollutants that are harmful to human beings. However, artists who have been working alone have been subjected to a variety of toxic fumes, powders, and chemicals. An organization was recently formed to dispense information to artists listing harmful materials that they may be using in their work. Dennis is solving a similar problem on his own.

Dennis Higgins designs the silver and gold settings for Carol Arnold's scrimshaw jewelry.

The design must be scaled down to the small surface before beginning. Remember this when choosing a design. You don't need lots of space for scrimshaw. Carol uses small drawers from an old chest for shelves to hold her inks. One of Mara Cary's baskets holds the ivory.

Because he is working primarily with ivory, he devised a way to divert the ivory dust which is harmful to breath and awful smelling. First, he built a safebox which looks like something out of a science fiction movie. The box is made of plywood, is table height, and large enough to hold a grinding wheel inside. The top is a pane of glass set into a wooden frame which is hinged at the back for easy opening. Each side has a hole which is large enough for his arms to slip into. Hanging from these holes are sleeves that have been attached at one end to each hole and elastic has been sewn around the outside of the other ends. These sleeves are made from the legs of old blue jeans. A small light is also rigged up inside. At the back of the contraption is another hole large enough for a vacuum cleaner nozzle to fit snugly when inserted. The vacuum sucks out the dust as the grinding wheel sands the ivory, and the other end of the vacuum sends the exhaust fumes out the window. Dennis can then put his arms inside the box through the sleeves, hold the ivory on the sandpaper that is attached to the top of the grinding wheel, and look through the glass top as he sands. On Nantucket where it is difficult to get supplies, you have to be more than creative; it helps to be downright ingenious.

Watching Carol do scrimshaw makes you feel that you want to rush home and try it. She makes it seem so easy. She is sure of herself when handling the tools. The interesting thing about Carol and scrimshaw is that she started doing it. Just like that. She didn't read books; there weren't any instructions at the time; she hadn't heard much about it; she didn't have any ivory when she first began; and she never watched anyone doing it. Carol is British and began doing scrimshaw in England on a cow bone. She told me that when she met Dennis he told her about scrimshaw so she tried it on cow bone. She said that when she started it was most difficult to remove all the meat from the bone. Had she had her dog, Luke, at the time, it would have been a lot easier, with Luke providing most of the labor.

Books are often used for design reference.

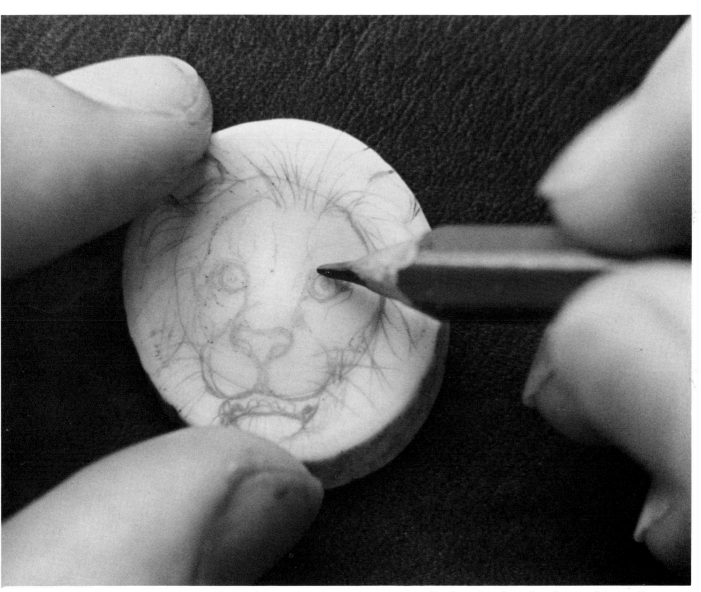

An expression on an animal's face is often hard to achieve. You may feel more comfortable tracing this kind of design. Carol draws the lion's head onto the disc using a soft pencil.

The black ink is applied first. This is the outline for the basic design
which Carol does first on all of her pieces.

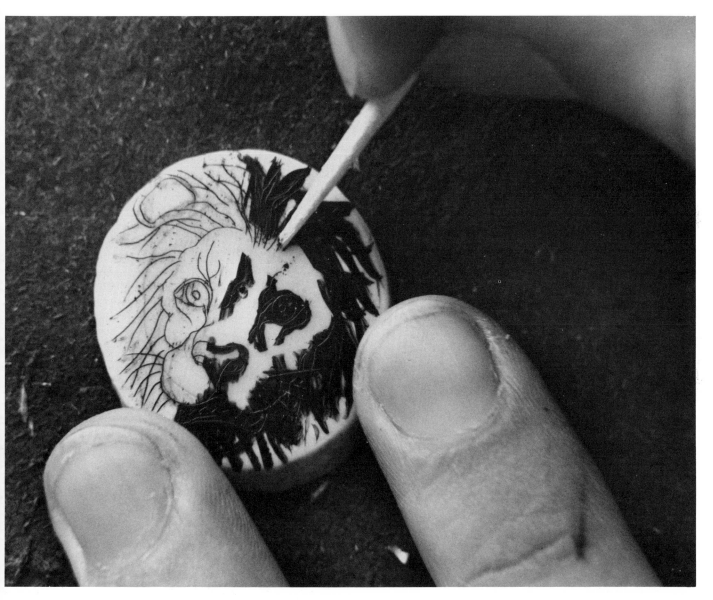

After the ink dries, Carol removes it with a little water on a toothpick. Actually running the toothpick over her tongue gives her the right amount of wetness without smearing the ink too much.

Once the ink is removed from the surface, Carol wipes it clean with a
dry rag. She prefers to allow the ink to dry before removing it to avoid
staining the ivory when using colors.

Carol continues to add engraved details. For each color there is a new set of lines. The mane is beginning to take shape here as well as the face. The hair is brown in color and the eyes are a bright emerald green. Since green often fades in sunlight, she made the eyes very bright.

At this point, the details have been completed. Using the scriber, Carol has added more and more shading, filling in with short close lines around his face. Notice that the nose has been engraved with many strokes and filled in with black ink. More hair has been added to fill out his mane. Go back and compare him to the original drawing. This is an interesting study in doing scrimshaw.

Using a jeweler's pliers or other handy tool, bend a piece of wire and clip off, leaving a small stem to be inserted into the drilled hole.

A small drill is used to make a hole in the top of the disc. Insert the wire and fill the hole with an epoxy glue. The scrimshaw should be set aside to dry for about thirty minutes.

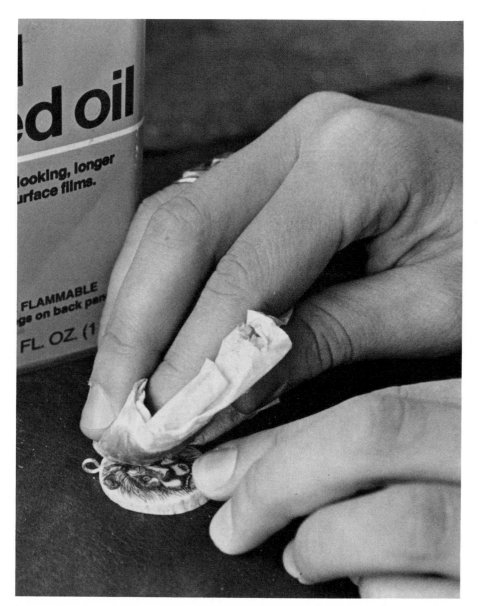

If you have worked on ivory, it should be rubbed with linseed oil. This prevents it from cracking and checking. The ivory has had the natural oil boiled out of it and must be preserved this way every six months. Bone, which is quite brittle, can be treated with linseed oil also.

This little jewel of a box is made from a whale's tooth and scrimshawed with a colorful, whimsical dragon by Carol Arnold. The lid is made of silver and gold by using the lost wax method of casting. The dragon on the lid is surrounded by butterflies and there is even one on his nose. This is the creation of Dennis Higgins, an accomplished metal smith and designer.

The inside of Carol and Dennis's box is simply a sanded-out indentation that looks like a thumb imprint. The little catch on the front is made of gold, and the lid is hinged.

Aside from his own necklaces and rings, Dennis has designed settings for Carol's scrimshawed neck pieces. One of the things that they did together, which I particularly love, is a small oval-shaped box. It is made from a whale's tooth; a small cavity is shaped out of the inside to form a space big enough for rings or other small treasures. Around the outside, Carol scrimshawed one of her whimsical dragons in the colors she is most known to use, pinks, reds, purple, and touches of green. The dragon has a butterfly on his nose. As if all this weren't enough, Dennis made a top for the box. It is made of silver and gold using the lost wax method of casting, and it is a replica of the dragon complete with butterflies. There is a tiny gold catch on the front. This box is the most exquisite little jewel you ever held in the palm of your hand.

Dennis has designed and made small boxes out of ivory that Carol has scrimshawed with delicate wildflowers. The combination of the pastel wildflowers and the clean white ivory of the hinged boxes is quite elegant.

Carol uses a dentist's tool to do her scribing. All her work is done in color using watercolor dyes. One of the distinctive things that she points out about her work is that she outlines all her designs with black ink. There is an outline to define every petal, stem, and blade of grass, and she scribes a black outline around her oval ivory pieces that set on the top of basket purses.

After applying the ink, Carol lets it dry, and then, using a piece of moist Kleenex, she rubs the excess ink off. The ink that remains on the surface and is not in the incised lines is scraped away with a toothpick. She lets the ink dry because if she rubs it away while wet, she runs the risk of having one color run into another or stain the surface. Since she uses fairly bright colors, it is not easy to prevent this without care. Once all the colors were on, Carol used to apply a coat of satin varnish over the entire design to protect it from fading or rubbing off.

She no longer does this as it ruins the ivory. Bill Sevrens, a fine craftsman in the art of making the famous Nantucket lightship baskets, works closely with Carol and many scrimshanders. He makes the baskets, and they supply the scrimshawed ivory piece that is placed on the top, further personalizing this prized possession. Bill clued Carol into using linseed oil to protect the scrimshaw from fading and eliminating the varnish. During our last visit, Carol told me that she was also switching fom watercolor dyes to oil paint. She was surprised to learn that the paint comes in so many vibrant colors, similar to the dye, and she felt that it had a more permanent quality. She is at an experimental stage with the materials; however, most scrimshanders are becoming loyal to either watercolor dyes or oil paint.

Carol Arnold's goal is to go on with her art education, and since she is expanding her artistic horizons, there is no telling where her talents will lead and what improvements and contributions she will make.

Carol is working on an elephant ivory plaque which will be applied to the top of a Nantucket Lightship basket. Resting the piece on a leather scrap, she outlines the oval.

Carol scribes all areas to be filled in with one color. Then, using a
pointed sable artist's brush, she fills in the scribed lines with Dr.
Martin's dye. The dye comes in small bottles and can be found in art
supply stores.

Working on one flower, Carol scribes, paints, and rubs off the dye until one design is complete. Sometimes it's necessary to add detail by going back to an area that has already been completed.

This close-up version of the plaque gives you a chance to see the detail that adds to the charm of Carol Arnold's designs. On the left, the grasses have been crisscrossed with black and the flower and mouse have been outlined with black. On the right side of the plaque the design has only been drawn but not yet scribed.

PLATE 108

ow, *Callirhoë involucrata*

Carol uses flower books for illustration reference to be sure that her flowers are accurate. Often she picks several blades of grass to find the one that most suits her needs. Looking at the natural way things grow is a good way to choose a design. There is inspiration everywhere.

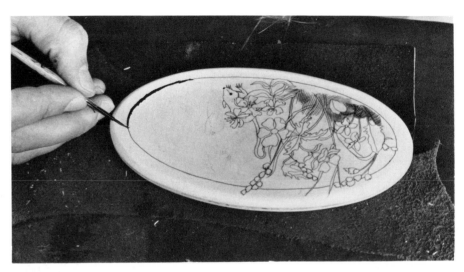

All of Carol's scrimshaw is outlined in black before she begins filling in with color. Every petal and leaf of the flowers as well as the blades of grass are accented with black.

Carol Arnold's scrimshaw has a casual uninhibited quality that is in keeping with wildflowers. If you study one of her flowers, it is a good way to start your own project. An entire scene would be too much for the beginner to attempt.

Here the design is finished with the flowers and leaves spreading over the oval outline for an added touch. Carol uses the colors of nature, sometimes making them brighter and cheerier than they actually are.

66

Robert Spring

Robert Spring is an accomplished illustrator and scrimshander. His scrimshaw has been in constant demand for he is a master of the craft. Bob's work is sold through the prestigious Four Winds Craft Guild which is owned by Morgan Levine, a knowledgeable collector of marine antiques and the grandson of a New Bedford whaler.

Bob uses old ships as his main subject, which is reminiscent of the scrimshaw that was done in the early days. However, his style is distinctive. If you study a detail of one of Bob's pieces, like a flag or a border, you will see that it is stylized as well as realistically rendered. His work has a recognizable quality that is not so evident in the old scrimshanders' work. That quality is complete sureness and control of line which gives him the flexibility to attempt more detailed subjects. He simply doesn't make mistakes.

Before meeting Bob I was curious about him. I had seen his work in person and in books, and I knew who he was. Why then was everyone always referring to him as the #16 man? When I watched Bob work, I understood. All this magnificent scrimshaw—curving lines of a flag, short quick strokes of water, long graceful lines of a ship—were done exclusively with a #16 X-Acto blade. When I finally met Bob, he said that he was sure that he had cornered the market on the #16 blade and that he alone was probably responsible for all of its sales. After hearing that, I was surprised that X-Acto hadn't renamed it the Robert Spring blade.

When Bob used to demonstrate his craft, people would ask him where they could buy that "scrimshaw tool," and I'm sure that many people who have seen Bob work still believe that the X-Acto knife was indeed made expressly for scrimshaw. When he holds that knife and begins to work you are sure of it also. But it is, of course, what he does with it. Firmly holding the knife with the blade turned away from the scrimshaw (the reverse of what you might expect), he just goes at it. It is incredible to watch, but he is so familiar and sure of his work that he does not need any drawing. Bob's entire rendering is done with the blade.

After scribing Bob applies oil paint with his finger. His pieces are mostly done using raw umber or burnt sienna, but he also uses brown, red, blue, or a combination of blue and brown for a sea green.

Living in Florida in the winter, Bob is surrounded with inspiration. His hobby is building ship models that are exact replicas of real ships. He has been working on his current model for two years—the cannon carriages having fifty working parts. An obviously patient man.

Bob discovered the X-Acto blade quite by accident. It was included in a kit that he used when he tried scrimshaw for the first time. He likes the subtle effect of the raw umber or burnt sienna oil paint, which he feels is most similar to the old scrimshaw. First, he suggests squeezing some paint right from the tube onto a piece of corrugated paper, such as the flap of a box. Leave this for about two hours so that the paper can absorb the excess oil from the paint. Sharpen the knife often for if it is allowed to get dull the incised lines will appear too solid and uneven when the paint is applied. Before beginning, Bob prepares his ivory or bone with varying grades of sandpaper; beginning with a #220 and progressing to #320, #400, and finally a #600. He does not use an electric sander when preparing a tooth. He does the entire preparation by hand, scraping and sanding away the ridges and unevenness of the surface until the clean white ivory appears.

A practice lesson

If you are inspired by the exquisite scrimshaw of Robert Spring and would like to take a lesson from him, you are in luck. Bob has devised a lesson for beginners, and he feels that if you want to do scrimshaw it is a good idea to practice the exercises again and again. He has a way of doing scrimshaw that is his own and that many people like. Now you can learn to do it his way. There are a few basic strokes that he uses on all his pieces. He has developed a decorative style of illustration and has attempted to simplify these basic strokes so that the newcomer can learn to do scrimshaw.

The cross-hatching is used for almost everything: borders, ships, and to fill in large areas. The scriber makes even scratches across the area to be filled in. The closer the engraved lines, the darker the area will be. Once these lines are filled in, you will draw the same-length lines across the other way, forming crisscrosses with your scribing tool.

Creating a curved line takes a bit more practice. Remember, you don't have to rush; it can and should be done slowly. A beginner should not simply pick up the knife and make a quick swirl. The use of the carving tool is more rigid and controlled than the use of a pen or paint brush. You can't just make a

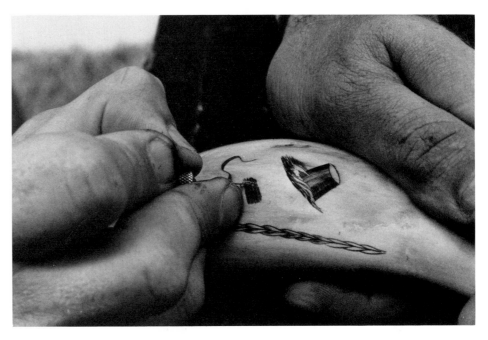

Notice the curved lines of the waves, the up and down lines, and the example of cross-hatching to the right of the S. The rope is a means for practicing lines, curves, and shading. The long stem of the leaves looks so graceful when Bob Spring does it, but this comes with experience. Do it slowly until the curved line flows evenly.

beautifully curved line with one stroke. Slowly draw the scriber around the material in order to form a graceful curving line. Turn the object as you go if this is comfortable. Do it over and over until the curve no longer looks halting and choppy. Keep doing this until you can do it with confidence.

Try scribing letters or a rope. This will give you a chance to practice different curves and strokes as well as filling in and shading areas. A great deal of pressure is applied to the tool in order to penetrate the material. If you scratch the surface only slightly, the ink or paint will not fill in. The rope is excellent to practice all the most frequently used techniques in scrimshaw. Bob says that the long line of a ship is the most crucial so take your time when doing this and first look at some examples. Study the effects you can create with the scriber. An X-Acto knife will give you good straight lines, but, unless you are as skilled as Bob Spring, you will need a less rigid tool for curved lines.

Now that you have practiced straight and curved lines and have successfully filled them in with paint, you can remove the entire lesson in ten minutes. With the knife blade or a pen knife or sharp kitchen knife, scrape away the work that you have done. That's right. Just scrape it away. After scraping, sand over the whole surface with several grits of sandpaper. Often scratches that were made are invisible. To avoid overlooking these, rub the surface until it is completely covered with the raw umber paint. Wipe off the paint and what scratches remain will now show up. Scrape these away to reveal a clean surface once again. Of course if you have been practicing on a shell, which is a good practice piece, just throw it away and look for another. Bone can be scraped and sanded just like the ivory. Use fine steel wool to polish the surface back to its original luster.

When deciding what kinds of lines are used for what subjects, keep in mind that curved lines are used for water or for flowers or a waving flag. Study the individual markings on the pieces shown in order to better understand how to scribe. The overall piece is inspiring and can give you design ideas, but it is best to look at one tiny section at a time in order to perceive the individual strokes.

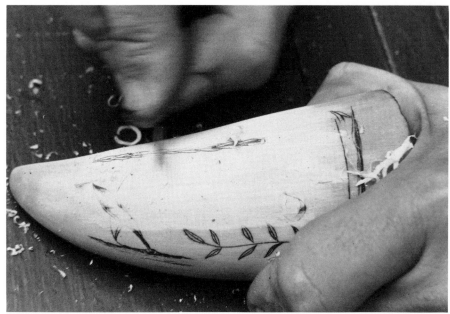

The entire lesson can be removed instantly by scraping it off with the blade or a penknife. Then sand over all, rub down with a #0000 steel wool, and begin again. If you've worked on a piece of plastic or a shell, throw it away. Bone can be sanded as ivory.

Many scrimshanders work with the Nantucket lightship basket makers, combining their talents. Here the party basket is made by M. Kane with ivory knobs and front catch. The ivory plaque is woven directly onto the top of the basket and scrimshawed by Robert Spring. Often the underside of the plaque is engraved with the owner's name. This ivory slab is made from elephant tusk.

The art of scrimshaw originated during our nation's early years by New England whalers who engraved and carved on whalebone and whale teeth the scenes that were most familiar to them. The whaling ship, the whales, and similar nautical motifs recorded the life of the sailor during the long voyages. Robert Spring, a modern day scrimshander, is influenced by the traditional scrimshaw, adapting it to his own decorative style. Engraved on this whale's tooth is the U.S.S. Franklin surrounded by a border which is typical of the old scrimshaw work.

Scrimshaw technique

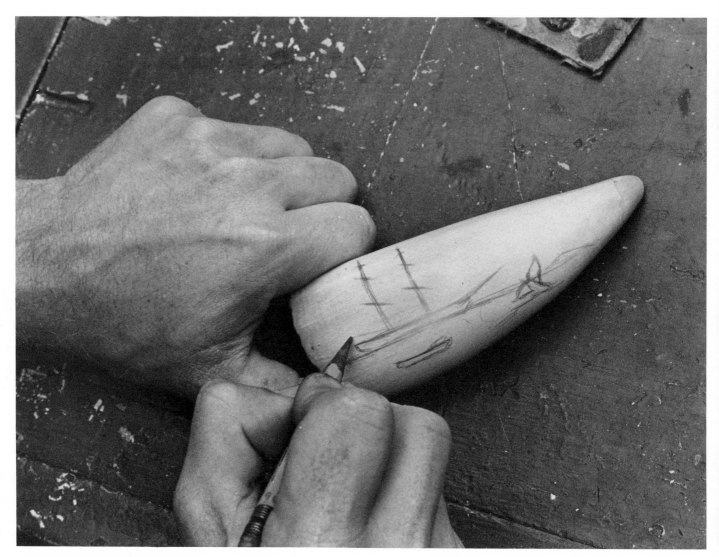

*Bob Spring does a quick pencil sketch before scribing with the knife.
For this piece he used no reference material.*

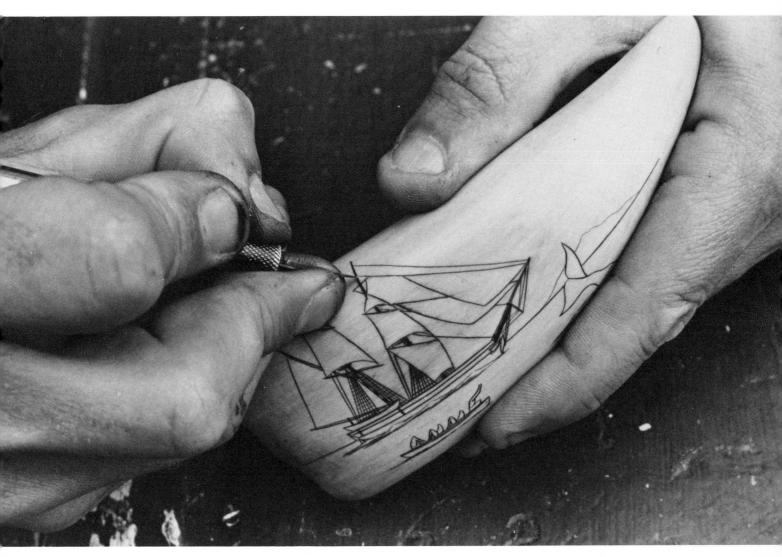

Holding the knife blade pointed away from the tooth, Bob Spring carefully presses into the tooth's surface. This is tense and exacting work, and the engraved lines must be precise when scrimshawing a ship. Bob is a master at this, having done it for many years.

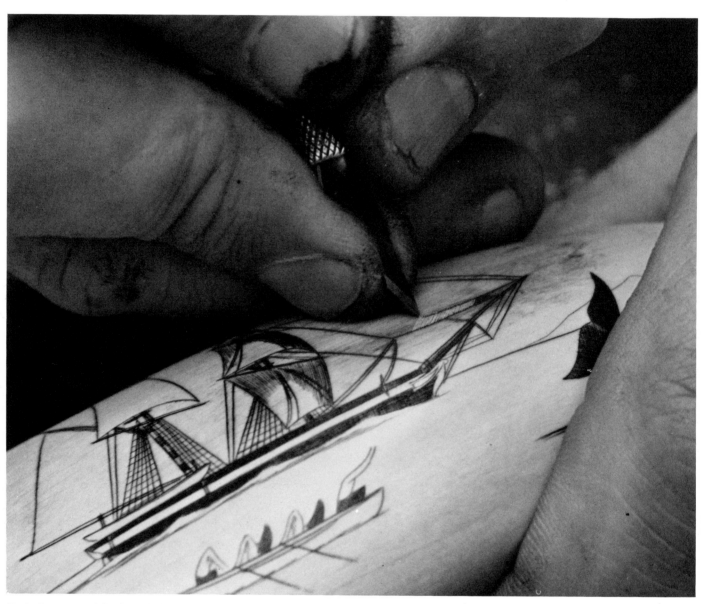

Bob Spring adds detailed lines to the ship. The heavy black areas on the hull of the ship and the whale's tail are made by scribing lines very close together and cross-hatching.

Using raw umber or burnt sienna oil paint, Bob rubs it into the engraved lines. This creates an effect similar to the old scrimshaw. His renderings are extremely realistic in every detail.

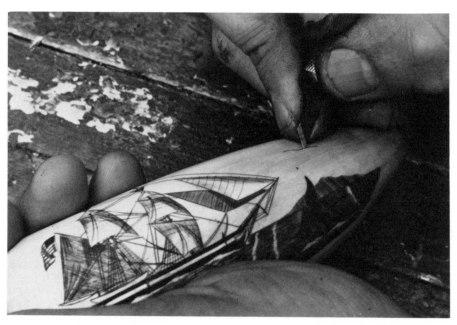

With a sweep of the knife blade, Bob engraves a delicate gull as a detail on his nautical scene.

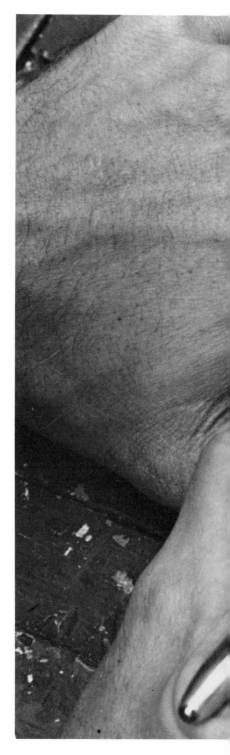

Bob puts the finishing touches on the scrimshawed scene that he has created with confidence and skill.

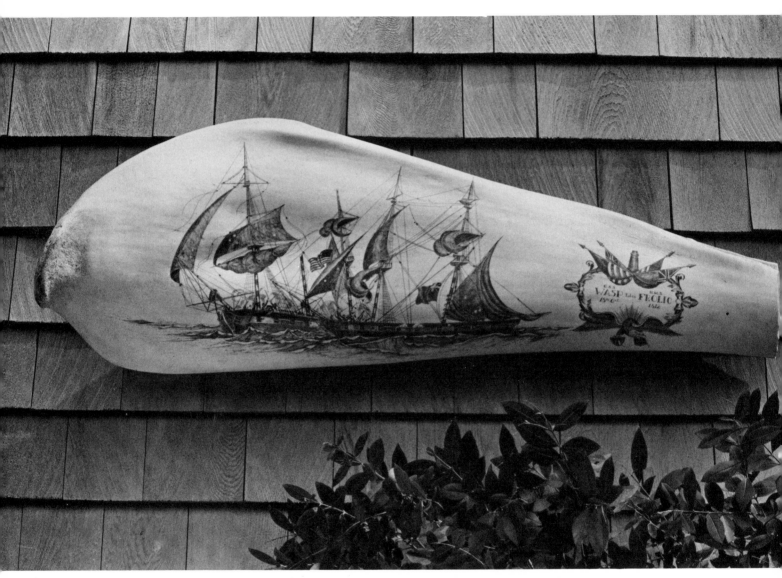

This pan bone, the rear part of a sperm whale's jaw, is approximately four feet long. The scene, the U.S.S. Wasp *taking the* H.M.S. Frolic, *is one of Robert Spring's most ambitious pieces.*

One of Robert Spring's outstanding pieces is a pan bone, the rear part of a sperm whale's jaw, which is scrimshawed with an incredible scene of the U.S.S. *Wasp* taking the H.M.S. *Frolic*. This pan bone is approximately four feet long, and Bob worked on it on the floor on his hands and knees. Study it to get a better feeling for the scribing technique and the individual markings. Perhaps you will never be a Robert Spring, but you can learn to do scrimshaw the way he does it. Bob has recently taught his wife, Donna, and although she leaves the ships to him, he claims that he could never do a shore bird as well as she does one.

This is a close-up view of a portion of the pan bone. Study all the details of the different lines and then practice his lesson. This will certainly give you a tremendous appreciation of his work.

A beginner tries scrimshaw

Peter Frey is a newcomer to scrimshaw. He was trying to figure out how to do crosshatching which is second nature to a seasoned scrimshander.

When I first met Peter Frey, he had just sailed to Nantucket from Barbados, a six-week voyage on his forty-foot sailboat. Peter has spent his life traveling around the world collecting marine antiques and had brought with him an unusual collection for his shop, The Shanty, located on the dock at Nantucket harbor.

While Peter is a seaman and has sailed all of his life, he had never heard of scrimshaw. One day a man came into his shop and offered him a pair of matching whale's teeth in exchange for a valued captain's chest. "What am I to to with those?" he exclaimed. "Scrimshaw them man!" was the reply. And that was the beginning of a new hobby for this German-born sailor.

One of the antique items in his possession was a rare vertibra disc. Peter's first try at scrimshaw was on the disc. It was bumpy and had a creviced surface, not at all conducive to scrimshaw. First he prepared it by filling in the holes and smoothing it out with wood putty. Then it was sanded. "My biggest problem," said Peter "was where to put the lines." Oh, if that were all.

Many scrimshanders have some basic knowledge of art and drawing which enables them to apply the scrimshaw carvings the way you would do a pen-and-ink drawing, engraving more heavily where the pen would add shading. Without this knowledge, Peter relied on old engravings and prints that he had in the shop. "I just studied the way ships were drawn and learned from that." One thing that he noticed when studying these paintings was that the wind was often blowing the sails in one direction and the flag would be blowing in the opposite direction. Peter said that he found this very humorous. His knowledge of ships of course gave him a head start in rendering sailing ships. The disc has an interesting primitive quality. Looking at basic art books is a good way to learn more about carving subjects for scrimshaw.

"I tried to find a scrimshaw tool, but I didn't know what to use," Peter lamented. "So I used what I had around the boat, an old sail needle and a marlin spike!" Of course, he didn't realize how close he was to the real thing.

A marlin spike can be found in most marine stores. It is a very sharp instrument used for undoing knots on a ship and is an excellent tool for scrimshaw.

Peter had a lot of trouble in the beginning because he didn't know where to put what—straight or curved lines. He wasn't sure about shading or how to get the desired effects. He looked at many paintings and drawings and checked basic drawing books to find out some simple ways to etch his lines. I suspect by next year Peter Frey will be an old hand at it.

Tucker Lindquist
Lesley Zaret
William Haffenreffer

Many scrimshanders are, like crafters everywhere, quietly working in their own special niche that they've made for themselves.

One day when the sun was shining, no clouds in the sky, a perfect day, Jon and I loaded the camera equipment into the car and took off to the outskirts of the island. We drove out through the moors until we couldn't go any further. Ahead of us was nothing but the ocean. The gulls made peaceful noises, the waves lapped over the shore, a more inspiring scene for scrimshaw was hard to imagine.

High on a cliff above the beach, completely isolated from other houses, a small beach house faced the ocean. This had become the summer studio for Tucker Lindquist, Lesley Zaret, and William Haffenreffer. Usually a crafter works alone, shut off from the outside world and people. This is a choice. The work is sometimes boring and tedious, but the crafter learns to deal with this. It is therefore an unusual treat to find a group of people who work together, each genuinely proud of the other's work. Their work blends nicely as do their personalities, yet their scrimshaw is individualized.

We had a lot of fun with these people, and we enjoyed our visits to photograph them working. The atmosphere was always pleasant, and it was easy to become friends while we talked and learned about how they did scrimshaw.

Tucker Linquist

In the winter, Tucker, Lesley, and Bill live and work in Amherst, Massachusetts, where they often take courses at the University of Massachusetts. Most of the time they work on their scrimshaw and sell their work at craft fairs in the area. These people are very conscious of their environment. They practice yoga, eat natural food, and when possible bike ride, swim, and surf. Scrimshaw seems to fit right into their way of living, providing a peaceful, creative way of earning a living. When Tucker is concentrating on his work, you feel that he is totally immersed in what he is doing, unaware of his surroundings. But this is not entirely true, for the atmosphere that they have created is deliberate. Their work and their lives are interrelated so that their work or play is enjoyable and fulfilling mentally, physically, and spiritually. Often I would hear Tucker use a word to describe his work in passing. I suspect that it is his word alone, and it certainly doesn't sound like someone going to work. He says, "I'm going to scrim."

When we first met Tucker, Lesley, and Bill they told us that we were in luck because they were on their way to a craft fair and had their best pieces to show us. Lesley said she was all scrimshawed out, having spent weeks preparing for the show. Bill felt he could have kept going. He likes to demonstrate the craft as he says people relieve the tension. Tucker is quite comfortable working alone, quietly concentrating on his work. When Tucker is showing people how it's done, he says someone will always ask, "Is that a decal?" They are simply unfamiliar with the craft.

Tucker Linquist was born on Nantucket and has always been familiar with scrimshaw. "I always had a piece of ivory in my pocket," he confided. "One day I just started doing it and have been ever since. For my birthday my parents and Bill sent me a box of ivory." Tucker's style has an interesting primitive quality. Sometimes there are tiny details that you almost have to use a magnifying glass to see. Often the dentine, that dark orange center of an ivory disc, becomes the focal point for Tucker's designs. Lesley and Bill began trying their hand, not wanting Tucker to have all the fun. So they got him to teach them.

Since Bill has had no art training, I asked him if he thought it was difficult to do scrimshaw without it. He said that he didn't think it was necessary and explained that many artists find it difficult to do scrimshaw because they are not working on a flat surface, and it is a tight style. While a person does not need to know how to draw, he must practice with the tools to master the technique.

"What about mistakes?" I asked. It seemed so permanent to make the wrong lines. I hadn't taken Bob Spring's lesson when I asked the question, but their answers were the same. Just sand it down and begin again.

Lesley confessed to many goofs and rejected pieces. There is a small vaselike pot in front of Lesley's work area. I looked inside,

William Haffenreffer

expecting to find some mysterious ingredient. "That's for my rejected ones," she said as she flipped a piece of ivory into it.

Asked about her choice of designs, Lesley said, "I can't do a piece that doesn't appeal to me. I have to like what I'm doing or the quality of the work is poor. If it's a flower that I am doing just to sell, strictly for commercial value, it never looks right." Lesley doesn't look at something, become awestruck and race home to scrimshaw it. Ideas come to her, and she creates a design from feeling. She told me that the nicest piece she ever did was so simple to do it was almost embarrassing.

A bookshelf in the corner of the living room held the familiar, well-worn books. Wildflower, bird, ship, and design books were some of the subjects used for inspiration. Bill showed me an old children's book that he said offered them an endless source of ideas. Sometimes parts of designs are used, often an entire design, and sometimes a design is even traced right from the original onto

Lesley Zaret

a piece of ivory. This is an excellent way to scrimshaw if you are not sure of your subject. Sometimes it is difficult to get a fix on the scale of an object in relation to the piece on which you are working. A tracing will help you judge beforehand. If you lay the traced bird or flower on your shell or other material you can tell if it will look well or too overpowering for the piece.

Left is a rough, bumpy shell that Linda Anne L'Abbé found on the beach and scrimshawed for a first try. It is really best to look for a smooth shell to make the work a bit easier. At right Linda prepares a natural-food dinner for Tucker, Lesley, Bill, and herself in the tiny kitchen of the beach house.

Linda Anne L'Abbé is the fourth member of the group. She is a novice scrimshander. How could she avoid it when she was surrounded with friends doing scrimshaw all day? During one of our visits to the beach house, Linda was in the tiny no-electricity kitchen where jars of interesting dried foods lined the walls, and a big barrel of apples took up a great deal of floor space. Fresh baked bread smells seeped from the oven. In the winter Linda takes classes and sews while living in Amhurst. "Do you do scrimshaw too?" I asked. "Nope, just scrimshelling," she replied.

"Scrimshelling" is Linda's way of doing scrimshaw. With art classes in her background, Linda is not a novice at drawing, and her first attempt at scrimshaw was delightfully done on a shell. "I thought I might scrimshaw a whole bunch of shells," she grinned impishly, "and put them back on the beach for people to find."

Tucker, Lesley, and Bill have found a method for creating unusual shapes for their ivory jewelry pieces. They keep turning and shaping until they are happy with each piece. Often a piece may take as long as thirty minutes before it is complete. Sitting in the sun shaping ivory is a pleasant experience when you're with friends.

The one aspect of their scrimshaw that Tucker, Bill, and Lesley are most proud of is that each of their pieces is hand shaped with great care. The design is then scribed to conform to the shape. For instance, if they are working with a round disc, they may sand the edges back and forth and around, working it until they have a piece that is shaped like a teardrop and rounded on all sides. A design that conforms to this new shape will then be scribed on it. The design is not determined until the shape is made. Sometimes a piece might have an interesting aspect to begin with. A hole in the center might suggest a tree trunk with a branch growing up and around the hole. The edges might be shaped and rounded to give the piece a soft shape and feeling. A large piece is sometimes reduced in size while shaping in order to allow a tiny design to be scribed on it. Some pieces are shaped into unusual dimensions. Nothing is wasted. Even the tiniest piece is used to make a little necklace for a small jewel of a design.

When a piece of ivory has a hole in the center or some other defect, you can work your design around it, making the imperfection an interesting detail. Here Lesley has scrimshawed the tree bending down around the hole. Notice also how the design conforms to the shape. This piece is the size of a small beef bone.

The shapes are used for jewelry, primarily necklaces. The finished items are often hung from delicate silver chains, but more often from a leather thong or velvet ribbon.

By our third visit, Jon and I were enjoying ourselves so much that we were thinking about taking up scrimshaw. Tucker said, "If you're going to write about scrimshaw you should try it." Lesley had previously given me a piece of ivory and an intaglio point, and I didn't want to tell them that I had been trying it. They may have asked for a look, and I wasn't ready to actually show it to anyone.

The water dripping on the whirling sandpaper keeps the dust under control as well as providing a sort of paste on the sandpaper which adds to the luster of the ivory. You have to get the feel for holding the piece just right so that your finger tips are not sanded raw.

That was the day they were shaping. There were clouds overhead and a fine mist in the air. Typical Nantucket weather. We couldn't tell if it would suddenly pour or the sun would miraculously appear. Bill moved over to take a break, and I began shaping with all five fingers getting in the way. The shaping is done on a reconstructed potter's wheel that is run by a foot pedal or rather knee pedal with power supplied by Tucker. The wheel has a piece of #220 3M Wet or Dry sandpaper attached to it with a wire rim. Just above the wheel is a water-filled plastic bottle with a small plastic hose attached to the bottle. This is secured in such a way as to allow drops of water from the bottle

to drip onto the sandpaper as the wheel revolves. This keeps the sandpaper wet so that the ivory dust is absorbed as the three scrimshanders sand and shape each ivory piece by holding it on the wheel and working it back and forth and all around, changing the shape. Each piece may take as long as twenty to thirty minutes. This is a pleasant experience because it is not so exacting as the other steps and does not require heavy concentration. This

A simple flower is a good project for a beginner. This delicate teardrop shape is perfect for the wildflower scrimshawed by William Haffenreffer. Bill recommends starting out with something a bit less detailed if you are trying it for the first time.

is also a great way to make unusually shaped pieces, although it can get monotonous unless you have good company, good music, or good thoughts to accompany you.

It is a good idea to do all your shaping at once while you are set up. The water dripping on the sandpaper and combining with the ivory dust creates its own paste and serves as a polishing compound so that you really don't have to polish the materials. A quick way to do this would be with an electric sander, but you run the risk of doing it too fast, cracking the piece or overdoing

Holding a piece of ivory just above the surface of the sandpaper, Bill
rounds off a teardrop-shaped piece that he has been forming. The edges
are nicely rounded and soft and sensuous to touch. Sometimes the piece
flies away from you if you don't have a firm grip on it.

This piece scrimshawed by Lesley Zaret has a domelike surface. Notice the detail of the ladder leaning against the tree.

it. You don't have as much control, and the results just aren't the same.

"There is only one hazard," they warned me. "Your fingers can get too close to the sandpaper and you'll lose a layer of skin."

"I'm fine, I can do it," I insisted.

"O.K. if you want to sand off all your skin go ahead, but you really should hold the piece so that your fingers don't touch the sandpaper," they told me. Every now and then Lesley would look up at Bill as if to say, "Well, we warned her. If she won't listen we can't help her."

It hardly looks difficult and the wheel goes around quickly so you don't immediately realize that you are slowly losing a layer of skin from your fingertips. However, I got the feel of how to hold the ivory just above the paper, but it took a bit of practice to keep it from spinning out of my hand.

The day ended and no one realized that it had started to rain. This was our last visit, and as we gathered up our things, Linda Anne arrived from her job in town. We said good-bye for the summer, knowing that we'd get together again, for Lesley, Bill, Tucker, and Linda had affected our lives in a very positive way. They are interested and growing, and their work is in a constant state of change. Their scrimshaw is good and getting better and best of all—unpredictable.

When crafters are open to change and learning and as they adapt new ideas to their way of working and living, it adds new dimensions to what they produce. We visited them again in Amherst, and I was surprised at the pieces they were working on. Now they were away from the ocean, and their new surroundings offered a different stimulation. Crafting is often dependent on this, and I suspect that these scrimshanders will continue to progress, improving the quality of their work. They live by an inner clock, and whether they are doing scrimshaw, studying, preserving foods, or making clothes, they bring each activity into harmony with the others.

Tucker is working on a primitive design that has all kinds of little details that are fun to find. Can you see the little person on top of the mushroom? Here the ink has been applied and the excess is being removed. It is taped to the paper for easy handling.

*The tiniest piece of ivory is used for this minute design. Perhaps it will
be a dainty necklace for a small child.*

Lesley's ivory buttons are about a half an inch in diameter. The symmetrical pattern is not an easy design to work when you are learning. The thread holes can be drilled with a small motor tool. If you do this kind of project, remember that scrimshaw should not be washed, so don't do buttons for something that will be put in the washer. Plastic and bone buttons are readily available and provide an excellent surface for scrimshaw.

Keeping the point of your scribing tool sharp is important. This is done on a wet sharpening stone.

Bird against the sun and waves was scrimshawed by Tucker Lindquist. This design is primarily orange and has an interesting quality because the center of the disc is slightly orange in color. It is 1½ inches in diameter.

Notice the soft rounded edge all the way around this oval disc. Bill shaped this disc which started out as a thick rather chunky piece. It took twenty minutes on the sanding wheel to create the new shape. Astrological signs are another suggested design idea.

Once the ivory is shaped following the natural circular lines, Tucker scrimshaws the design to conform to the new shape. Here he has used the orange center, known as the dentine, to emphasize the flower design. This is a popular theme for his necklaces, which are quickly sold through local shops on Nantucket and in Amherst, Massachusetts.

Lesley's snowflake design matches the buttons and is "scrimmed" in one color. Often a rich color is quite elegant against the white.

This is an entirely different style for Tucker and one you might like to try. Do this slowly so that your outline does not look choppy. The disc is about 1½ inches in diameter.

Larry Vienneau

One of the larger gift shops on Nantucket is also a major supplier of scrimshaw material for the island crafters as well as the hobbyist who would like to try it. They carry the finished work of a handful of scrimshanders, as well as offering the customers the opportunity to see scrimshaw demonstrations regularly. Many people have walked casually into the store just to observe and have left armed with the materials for a newly discovered hobby. They have been inspired by the skill and ease which Larry Vienneau brings to scrimshaw.

Larry, a college student, has been demonstrating his craft since he first began doing it in high school, following an accident in 1970 when Larry broke his neck. Larry works primarily on whale's teeth and up until recently his theme was that of whaling days, ships and related nautical scenes. He can hardly keep up with the demand for his work, the sale of which has put him through art school.

The tiny island of Nantucket has a year-round population of approximately 4,500 but swells to 35,000 each summer. For over four years, Larry has had a steady stream of observers and says he has probably heard every imaginable question asked about scrimshaw. Considering that whaling has not been practiced in Nantucket for over one hundred years and that most of the people in this country have become enlightened about protecting endangered species, Larry was taken back when asked the following question. A little old lady had been watching him work for quite awhile. She had asked him several questions about what he was doing. Finally she said, with some obvious awe, "Did you harpoon the whale yourself?"

Larry, when first learning scrimshaw, was influenced by the work of Robert Spring. He still uses the X-Acto knife but instead of a #16 blade finds a #11 more to his liking. He does all his sanding by hand and uses the steel wool for a final polishing. He sharpens his blade with a lubricated stone. He has an old cloth that he has been using to wipe off ink ever since he started, and it is black with use. When Larry is working in the store, he uses a small high intensity lamp which allows him to see where he's scribed, better than under natural light. He says that each scratch breaks the light reflection, and he can tell what he has already done.

Inspired by the old scrimshanders, many of Larry's designs are emphasized with a decorative border. He usually begins by scribing the border as a setting for his nautical scenes. He crosshatches around the base and tip of a tooth. Then he sketches in his scene roughly. From this rough sketch, he begins the patient, laborious scrimshaw process.

Larry Vienneau

You can really get a feel for the size of the tooth here. Most teeth of the sperm whale average from four to ten inches although the largest was reported to be eleven inches. This rendering of the whaler Essex *is an excellent example of the fine artistry and craftsmanship of Larry Vienneau's scrimshaw.*

Larry Vienneau keeps up with art classes and has had a talent for drawing all his life. While he uses ships as his main theme most of the time, he has recently expanded his ideas and now uses varied and intricate designs to express his talent further. Where do his ideas come from? Mostly in odd moments, he says. Sometimes he is just daydreaming and an idea pops into his head. Other times he has a plan and carefully works it out on paper before commiting it to a tooth. Most scenes are sketched over and over on paper until they are just right and then they are often worked out again so that they will be the right scale for the object on which it will be scribed.

One of the teeth that Larry scrimshawed had a decay in one side of it. It was quite a large hole and rather grotesque. Instead of discarding this tooth, he used the decayed area in his design, incorporating it into a bizarre scene. Later he had a jeweler embed a stone in the cavity. The entire piece has an interesting and unusual quality.

As an art student, Larry experiments with varied designs. This head of Medusa is an unusual design for a scrimshaw theme. Notice the basic cross-hatching technique used throughout this design.

Some time ago Larry was commissioned to scrimshaw a whale's tooth with the U.S.S. *Constitution*. He first sketched it roughly, then began scribing, doing most of the detailed work with the #11. When he had finished, this piece represented twenty-five hours of work. He sat back to admire it before delivering it to the man who had ordered it. He noticed that one of the rigging lines was not quite touching one of the masts. He began to carefully touch it up. Then his knife slipped, gouging across the entire tooth. In no way could this mistake be resanded and the scrimshaw saved. Twenty-five hours wasted. There was only one thing to do; he redid the entire thing. That is one piece of scrimshaw he will never forget.

When scrimshawing a scene with several ships, Larry suggests sketching all the hulls first, then all the masts, rather than sketching one ship completely and moving on to the next. In this way you will be able to plan the scene so that it fits well on the object. He leaves the water until the last and uses short curved strokes to indicate the waves.

This fantasy design is a creation that Larry first worked out on paper. He made many sketches before actually committing it to the ivory. One of the outstanding aspects of his work is that the designs completely surround the object. He takes into consideration the sides and back as well as the front.

This is the back side of the Wizard tooth. Notice the tree wrapping around and the leaves turning into the fish that the wizard is trying to hook. The entire design is integrated, and one has to look again and again to find details that are often overlooked.

One of the interesting things about Larry's designs is that he takes the entire object and works with it as a whole. Rather than limiting his scrimshaw to one side, as if it were a painting done in two dimensions, he often has his designs wrap around the tooth and continue on all sides so that it is completely three-dimensional.

Larry Vienneau's scrimshaw is exciting and diversified, and often when you study one of his pieces, you will find a detail that you overlooked before—a pleasant surprise.

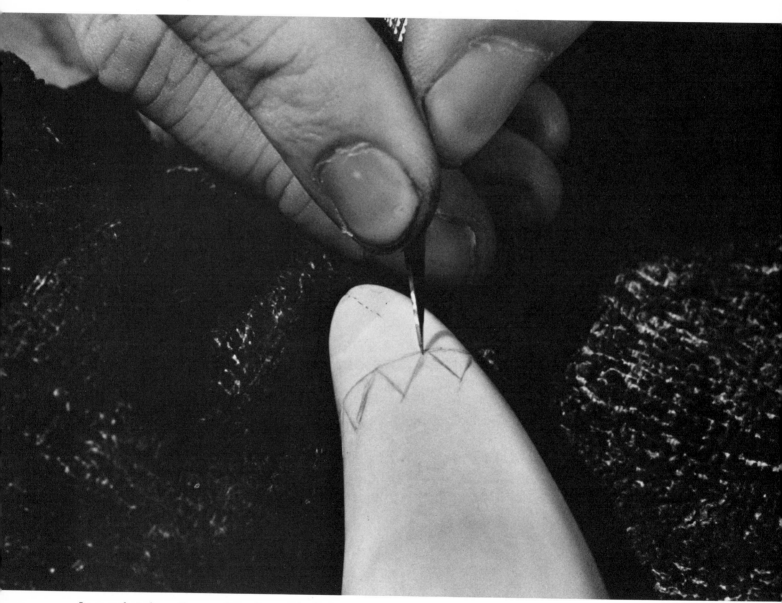

Larry sketches, then scribes the outline of the border before filling in the lines. A great deal of pressure is applied to penetrate the surface so that the paint will fill in sufficiently.

Larry Vienneau uses a #11 blade for an X-Acto knife. Influenced by the old scrimshaw of whaling days, he usually decorates his teeth with a border of cross-hatching. Here he has applied oil paint to the engraved lines. He does two or three sections at a time before going on.

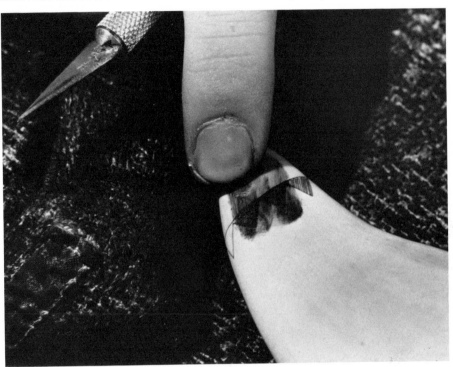

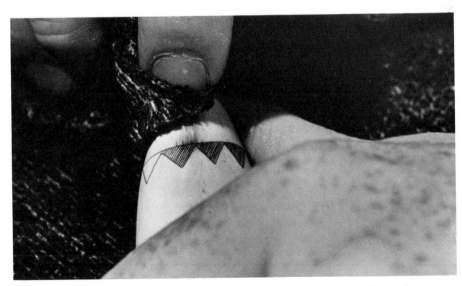

Using a soft rag, Larry wipes away the excess paint. If the lines are close together, the area will be quite dark. First, lines are engraved one way, then they are scribed close together going the other way, crossing those that were first scribed. This is known as cross-hatching.

Richard Peterson at work in his studio overlooking acres and acres of salt marshes and wildlife. Dick lives in the house that he built on Nantucket.

Richard Peterson

Richard Peterson is an established artist. His oil paintings and watercolors are in collections throughout the country. One of the notable things about Dick as an artist is his versatility. His oils are abstractions, and his watercolors are a unique blend of abstraction and realism. The flavor of his work is both oriental and nature oriented at the same time. The delicacy of his line work is reminiscent of oriental drawings. There is a quality of freeness in his exuberant washes combined with his delicate line drawings that represents a style that belongs to this artist and is consistent in everything he does. There is a spontaneity that comes naturally to him, and it is inherent in his work. Dick and his wife, Sabra, own the oldest private art gallery on Nantucket's South Wharf, where they exhibit the innovative work of many crafters and artists.

If you could stand in Dick's studio over a period of a year and look out at the endless salt marshes, you could see an incredible variety of birds and wildflowers. He brings all of this background to bear on scrimshaw when he does it. His scrimshaw, frequently a nature theme, has certain qualities not often found in other crafters' work. There is a delicacy and fluidity of line that is rarely seen in scrimshaw, past or present. His birds and flowers have that rare combination of qualities. They are composed or designed in a refreshing manner, yet they are also accurate and extremely realistic.

When creating scrimshaw jewelry, Dick Peterson looks at each project as a new challenge. He combines creative curiosity with artistry and craftsmanship that usually results in the unexpected.

We visited Dick at his studio which is located several miles from town and isolated from the everyday activities. His paintings were everywhere. In a corner was a small desk which held all the scrimshaw material. While he worked on scrimshaw, he told us that he was preparing for a one-man show of his work. Today he had turned from his painting to finish up a piece that he had been scrimshawing so that it would be ready in time. Boxes were piled here and there holding precious pieces of ivory.

This lightship basket plaque by Dick Peterson is made of elephant ivory. The scrimshawed scene illustrates the delicate touch with which Dick creates the birds and salt marshes for his scrimshaw as well as his watercolor paintings. The close-up at the bottom of the page allows you to study the individual engraved detail to further appreciate the fluidity of lines which is so characteristic of this artist's work.

When we arrived, Dick was working on a plaque for the top of a lightship basket. The subject, a favorite with Dick, was birds in flight. From his window, we could see his daughter's beautiful horses grazing in the distance, another subject for Dick's scrimshaw.

One of the distinguishing aspects of Dick's scrimshawed jewelry is unusual shapes. His pieces are essentially two-dimensional, and he experiments with large sculptured neck pieces. The scrimshaw is only one element of his intriguing pieces. The ivory shapes that he creates are often formed from

slabs with rough edges which become part of the design. One of the more unusual shapes that he has created lends itself to the butterfly design that is scrimshawed on it, and the delicate silver setting is interrelated to add yet another dimension.

Another of his creations is a bracelet made up of six or seven ivory discs linked together. Each disc is individually scrimshawed with a different wildflower or seashell. These bracelets are made from a whale's tooth. The narrow end is used so that the small discs are similar in size. Each disc is sketched and scrimshawed separately as if it were a complete piece. However, while each is a

The wildflowers of Nantucket are a favorite theme with Dick as well as with the people who wait months for the bracelet they have ordered. The idea for this piece is a good example of the creative experimentation that this artist brings to his work. Each of these projects is looked at as a new challenge and no two are exactly alike. Often Dick will leave one of the discs blank so the purchasers may choose the flower of their choice for the remaining one.

complete illustration by itself, it must also relate to the others so that when the individual pieces are linked together they will complement one another. In order to keep them in perspective, Dick lays them side by side on a piece of masking tape. Then he plans out the entire bracelet and does a pencil sketch on each one. After that he scribes and finishes each disc before going onto the next. Two small holes are drilled in the sides of each one, and the discs are linked together with brass rings.

The scrimshaw technique is second nature with Dick, and many beginners flock to his gallery to study his style. I have heard other crafters say that Dick Peterson does the finest scrimshaw ever seen. When he picks up his scribe and begins to work you want to hold your breath. He is like an accomplished diamond cutter at work. He is sure and confident, and his work is delicate and restrained.

As an artist he has the ability to do a rough sketch and from there go right into the scribing, achieving incredible detail. He told me that the engraving is tedious because of the tremendous pressure that must be applied.

"Why doesn't the ink wear off after awhile?" I asked.

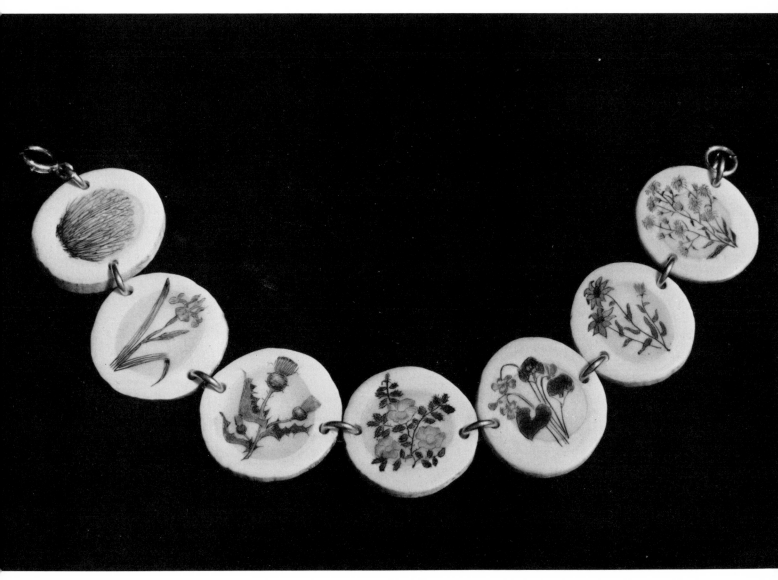

This seven disc ivory bracelet is an original creation of Dick's and only three or four are made each year.

This bracelet is made up of five discs that were cut from the end of a whale's tooth. It is a creation of Dick Peterson's. The seashell design is first sketched onto each disc before it is scribed. While each disc must be a complete design, it also relates to the whole. The holes are drilled on the sides of each disc so that they can be linked together to form the bracelet.

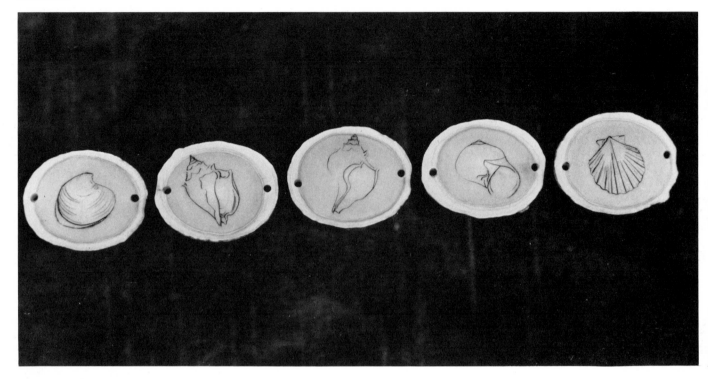

"The ivory is extremely porous and once the lines are scribed, the ink fills the scratches and soaks into the tooth or piece of ivory. This prevents the design from rubbing off with use. If the ink comes off as you scribe because your hand rubs on the areas that you have completed, then you aren't applying enough pressure when you engrave the lines. This is easy to correct," he told me. "You simply have to redo those areas and apply more pressure, engraving a deeper cut."

Dick uses watercolor dyes and wipes away the excess with alcohol. He does not wait for the dye to dry once it is brushed on. He simply applies the color and wipes it away from the surface leaving the ink or dye that has seeped into the scribed areas. A sharp tool resembling those belonging to a dentist is his primary scriber.

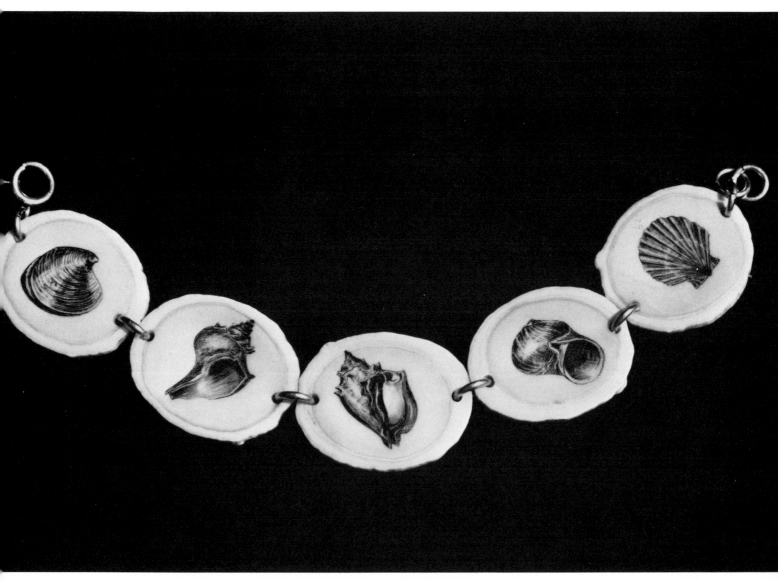

Here the bracelet is finished. The scrimshaw is done with watercolor inks in very subtle colors that represent the actual color of shell. Dick sketches all the discs before scribing. However, once he begins to engrave the lines, he completes each disc before going onto the next. In this way he is sure that each one is related to the one he has just finished.

Being at Dick Peterson's studio made me feel that he was very close to doing things the way those early scrimshanders had done. After all, they were insulated on a ship, and their only inspiration for scrimshaw, other than their memories or daydreams, was their environment. Quite naturally they drew scenes of nautical life. Dick is living on an island. His studio seems remote. And he's using his environment for inspiration, scrimshawing what he sees in his world—the birds, the wildflowers, and salt marshes that surround him. It provides a romantic setting for a modern-day scrimshander.

A scrimshawed ivory piece shows a hawk with fish. The unusual jagged edge piece of ivory is often used by Dick Peterson. Using these shapes adds another dimension to his work. Often the simplicity of the uncluttered design is what makes it more attractive. The beginner is often tempted to overdo the decoration.

Unusual earrings scrimshawed by Dick Peterson are typical of his imaginative style.

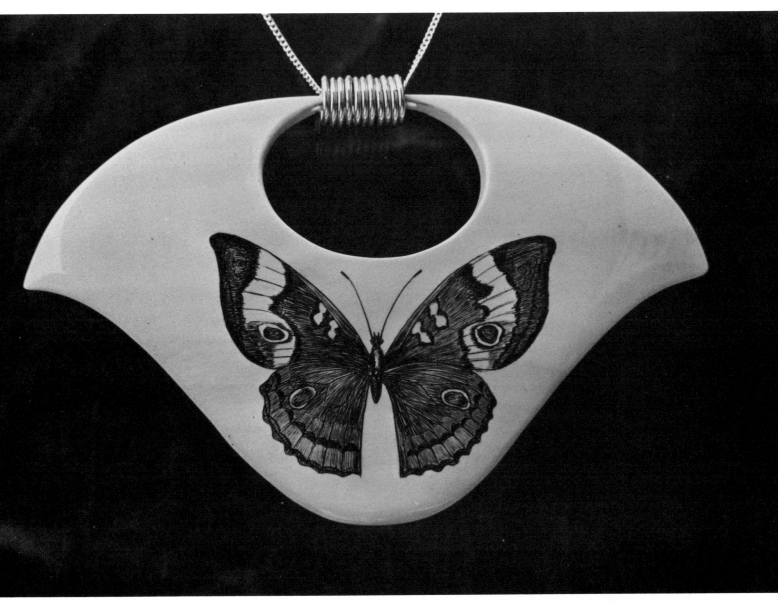

Richard Peterson's sculptured neck pieces are a fine example of this artist's ability to combine unusual shapes with related designs. The scrimshaw, its shape, and the silver rings all combine to give this piece a unique quality.

Ivory

Ivory is disappearing in this country. Whale ivory will no longer be available in a few years. Elephant and walrus ivory is becoming as scarce. Crafters who use ivory for carving and for scrimshaw will eventually have to turn to substitute materials. Many already have.

The use of ivory dates back to prehistoric days and has been used for decorative objects and carvings ever since. Used primarily as a decorative material, ivory was carved or incised and for some periods of history, provides the only graphic records we have.

Ivory is not as brittle as bone. The pores are close and compact and filled with an oily solution. This contributes to the polish and makes it more pliable to the carver or scrimshander. Some elephant tusks are as long as ten feet and weigh up to 180 pounds. Half of the tusk is hollow, therefore it must be used in a different manner than the solid part. In the Museum of Natural History in New York, there is a tusk which is thirteen feet long, two feet in diameter and weighs 220 pounds.

In the twelfth and thirteenth centuries, artists used ivory to carve religious figures. Hippopotamus teeth and walrus tusks were also used extensively for ivory carvings. While historically ivory was used by artists strictly for decorative items, it was more practically used in modern times for cane and umbrella handles, letter openers, chess sets, silverware handles, and fans. To this day, billiard balls are made of ivory.

Ivory was used in all countries for centuries. Queen Victoria sat on an ivory throne. In England, candlesticks were made of ivory, and we have examples in museums today of the religious art that was carved in ivory in the thirteenth, fourteenth, and fifteenth centuries. Carvings of religious statues were done with much attention paid to accurate detail. Early ivory caskets were decorated with figures carved in relief. There were also mirror cases, combs, and other personal items made of ivory which were not confined to the church.

An elephant tusk can be as long as ten feet and weigh up to 180 pounds. While elephants are not yet on our endangered species list, this source of ivory is scarce. These slabs are used for the plaques on the lightship baskets as well as for pendants and buckles.

A prevalent form of decoration throughout the fourteenth century in most western countries was done on small boxes, writing tablets, and combs. Early in the fifteenth century bone was frequently used in Italy as a substitute for ivory, and most bone carvings of this time are Italian. Even then, ivory was becoming scarce and costly.

In the seventeenth and eighteenth centuries snuff was popular. It was not sold ready-made and had to be grated for use. There were people who went from house to house with tobacco graters to offer this service. These early tobacco graters were made of ivory as were the many individual and often elaborate snuff boxes.

While chess sets have been made of all kinds of material for as long as the game has been known, some of the finest chess pieces have been made of ivory. Ivory has also been used for sword and dagger handles as well as other weaponry.

As I have mentioned, the supply of whale ivory in this country is now limited to whatever material suppliers had purchased from other countries before it was illegal to do so. When this supply has been exhausted, and at present it is primarily limited to seaport towns, there will be no more whale's teeth or bone in this country. At the present time, scrimshanders must, according to law, purchase their material in the state within which they work and sell their wares. Therefore, if you would like to do scrimshaw on a whale's tooth or whalebone, you must buy it in your own state, make it there, and keep it or sell it in your state. If, however, you would like to purchase the work of a particular scrimshander, you must go to where that person is in order to purchase one of that scrimshander's works. You may then take it home with you to another state if it is for your own personal enjoyment and not for resale.

All the scrimshanders who I have talked to and perhaps all scrimshanders are concerned with saving the whale as an endangered species. The uninformed person is often horrified to see a scrimshander working on a whale's tooth, convinced that the crafter is promoting the killing of whales. This could not be further from the truth. The work that is now being done, is significant. In the next several years, all scrimshaw work done on whale ivory and whalebone will be the last scrimshaw pieces produced in the United States on this material. No one knows how much of a supply is left, but the scrimshander is aware with each piece that is made, that it is one of the last pieces of scrimshaw done in this country. The scrimshander is scrimshawing with great care, knowing the precious value of the whale's tooth being worked. Scrimshaw as part of our American heritage will some day soon no longer be done on ivory.

Scrimshaw Art Preservation Act

S.229 is a bill which was referred to the Committee on Commerce. The purpose of the bill is to amend the Endangered Species Act of 1973 so that it will be consistent with the Marine Mammal Protection Act of 1972. S.229 is designed to preserve the art of scrimshaw. Due to the prohibitions of the Endangered Species Act of 1973, artisans are now forbidden from selling their finished scrimshaw products in interstate commerce. While other materials could be used, most scrimshanders have not had sufficient time to adapt their craft to other sources. Thus, in order to assure the preservation of this art form, S.229 permits the Secretary of Commerce, who administers the Endangered Species Act with respect to whales, to grant exemptions for a limited period of time for the sale of finished scrimshaw products in interstate commerce. This legislation would permit scrimshanders sufficient time to both dispose of their present inventories and to adapt their art to a new medium, without encouraging an endless trade in products of endangered species.

The Marine Mammal Protection Act, which was passed by the Congress on October 21, 1972, was designed to prevent the further slaughter and depletion of marine mammals throughout the world by removing the United States' market for the parts and products of these mammals. The act prohibited the importation and sale in interstate and foreign commerce of such parts and products, although these prohibitions did not apply to marine mammals taken prior to December 21, 1972, the effective date of the act.

Congress passed the Endangered Species Act of 1973 which strengthened its 1969 predecessor by prohibiting not only the importations but also the sale of endangered species and their parts and products in interstate and foreign commerce. Unlike the Marine Mammal Act, however, the Endangered Species Act contains no retroactive exemptions for the interstate sale of parts and products of endangered marine mammals which were legally held under the 1972 Act. This inconsistency has resulted in a great deal of confusion in the enforcement of the laws and has created financial hardship for scrimshanders and other artisans who deal in carved whalebone and teeth. These individuals possess substantial inventories of legally acquired whalebone and teeth used in their craft but are prohibited from marketing their finished products under the 1973 act. Since exemptions for the sale of these art objects cannot be granted administratively, legislation is needed to rectify the situation.

On January 17, 1975, Sen. Edward M. Kennedy (Democrat–Massachusetts) and Sen. Edward R. Brooke (Republican–Massachusetts) introduced S.229. The bill was referred to the Senate Commerce Committee. After a comment period during which the public was asked to express its views on the bill, the Senate Commerce Committee reported an amendment to S.229 in the form of a substitute bill.

The amended version of S.229 sets forth more clearly the intent of Congress in enacting the legislation, that is, to preserve the native American art of scrimshaw, but not to promote or perpetuate the trade in products of endangered species. The committee views this legislation as providing a transition period during which scrimshanders may sustain themselves through the marketing of their finished products in interstate commerce, while at the same time adapt their art to other media which are legal for interstate sale.

S.229, the Scrimshaw Art Preservation Act of 1975, has, at the time of this writing passed the Senate, but is awaiting approval from the House Committee on Merchant Marine and Fisheries.

Designs for reference

When starting a project, it is often helpful to have design suggestions. There are several books that are excellent for design subjects. Some of these designs can be traced from the books, others are good reference material. I have selected designs that could be suitable for scrimshaw. They can be used exactly as they are or for reference. Perhaps you will want to use part of a design, or you may decide to trace one of them and use it exactly as it appears. Most of the designs used here are from the Dover Pictorial Archive Series. This is an excellent source of picture material for commercial artists and designers. On a variety of subjects, these books are also of value to the crafter looking for design ideas. The designs selected for this book, however, are only from a few of these books. On the opposite page is a list of all the titles so that if there is a particular subject that you are interested in you will know if it is available.

Alphabets and Ornaments
Art Deco Designs and Motifs
Art Nouveau and Early Art Deco Type and Design
Baroque and Rococo Pictorial Imagery
Baroque Cartouches for Designers and Artists
The Book of Signs
Catchpenny Prints, 163 Popular Engravings from the
    Eighteenth Century
Chinese Folk Design
Classical Ornament of the Eighteenth Century
Costumes of the Greeks and Romans
Decorative Alphabets and Initials
Decorative Art of New Guinea
Designs and Patterns from North African Carpets
Devils, Demons, Death and Damnation
Early Illustrations and Views of American Architecture
Early New England Gravestone Rubbings
Geometric Design and Ornament
Handbook of Designs and Devices
Handbook of Early Advertising Art
Handbook of Ornament
Handbook of Plant and Floral Ornament
Illustrations of Heraldic Crests
Japanese Design Motifs
London Tradesmen's Cards of the Eighteenth Century
Montgomery Ward and Co. Catalogue, 1895
An Old-Fashioned Christmas in Illustration and Decoration
Optical and Geometrical Patterns and Designs
Ornamentation and Illustration from the Kelmscott Chaucer
Pictorial Calligraphy and Ornamentation
Pueblo Designs
Three Classics of Italian Calligraphy
A Treasury of Design for Artists and Craftsmen
200 Decorative Title Pages
Symbols, Signs and Signets
Victorian Stencils

These designs are from Pattern Design *by Archibald H. Christie and represent a sampling of over 400 illustrations. These patterns may be adapted to borders for scrimshaw, or you might want to incorporate parts of them into your main design. The flowers appear quite large here but could be reduced to fit onto a small object. These are simple patterns that can be adapted for scribing.*

From Symbols, Signs and Signets by Ernst Lehner, 1,350 illustrations of signs and symbols make excellent subjects for scrimshaw. Only a few are presented here in order to give you an idea of what's available. A personal sign or symbol, such as a family crest, is another subject that could be drawn and scribed. Some of them are simply outlined, and you will have to decide where to apply the necessary engraved lines. Others, such as the apple, suggest where you might fill in and shade.

Selected from A Source Book of French Advertising Art, *George Braziller, Inc. 1964, the old engravings of ships do not have any particular meaning, but they can help you sketch and scribe a ship. Studying old engravings is a good way to learn how to draw these subjects for scrimshaw. A favorite subject with today's scrimshanders, ships are found on much of the scrimshaw being made in sea towns. Aboard whaling vessels, the original scrimshanders used their own ships as models, and today we find historic ships adorning many scrimshawed whale's teeth.*

Art nouveau designs are often used for all kinds of craft work. These designs from Art Nouveau, An Anthology of Design and Illustration from the Studio *show you how the use of letters can be combined with decorative flowers. You might scribe the group of flowers just as they are. This might be the perfect subject for your first colorful scrimshawed piece. Remember, if the design is not the right size for your project, check the instructions on how to scale it to the size you need.*

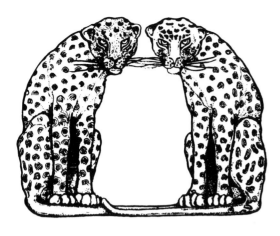

These art nouveau designs come from a delightful book of ornaments by artists Alphonse Mucha, Maurice Pillard Verneuil, and Georges Auriol. This book might be worthwhile to purchase because it is completely in color. The colors are beautifully subtle and might be inspirational when selecting the colors for your scrimshaw project. Mucha designed posters, calendars, stained glass windows, and many more of his designs can be adapted to scrimshaw. Art Nouveau Designs in Color, Dover Publications, New York, is a paperback book with sixty full-color plates for $4.00.

These are more signs from Symbols, Signs and Signets *which lend themselves perfectly for pendants or, perhaps, a key chain disc.*

The small primitive designs represent a sampling of popular engravings from the eighteenth century. They are rather crudely drawn, however, some of the subjects can be adapted to a first project. For instance, you may want to use the illustration of a small bird on a branch for reference. You could draw your own scene, using this composition idea. The engraved lines may help you to place the scribed lines on your scrimshaw piece. This book, Catchpenny Prints, contains 163 popular engravings from the eighteenth century and is part of the Dover list.

Redstart

Ox eye Titmouse

Wood Lark

Wren

Grasshopper Lark

Lamb

Eagle

Ape

Linnet

Bear

Nightingal

Buck

Chafinch

Hedge Hog

Tulip

Hound

Stork

Crow

Tyger

Ship

Mackarel

French Horn

Cherry Tree

Sparrow

Greyhound

Raven

Turkey

Mouse

Goose

Greenfinch

Duck

Bull Dog

Wryneck

Lion

Rabbet

These marvelous designs are selected from A Book of French Advertising Art. If you look carefully at each design, you will get a good feeling for where to scribe your lines. You might even want to study them under a magnifying glass.

The symbols here are from American Indian Design and Decoration, *LeRoy H. Appleton, Dover Publications, and are but a few of the 700 illustrations contained in this book.*

The stylized florals are from A Treasury of Design For Artists and Craftsmen consisting of 725 paisleys, florals, geometrics, folk and primitive motifs by Gregory Mirow. Their delicate quality makes them quite adaptable for scrimshaw designs.

Typography books are a good source for studying different type styles. Choose a style that you like but also that you feel you will be able to scribe successfully.

ABCD
EFGHIJKLMNO
PQRSTUVW
XYZ
12345&67890

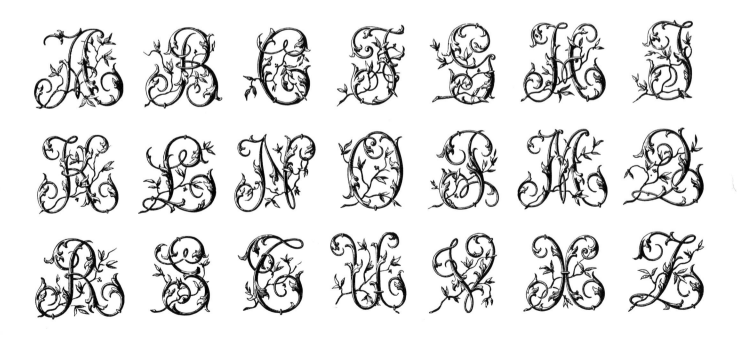

Many scrimshanders use decorative letters when signing their names to a piece. However, as a main subject, an initial can be scribed quite elaborately, incorporating flowers or other decorative ornamentation.

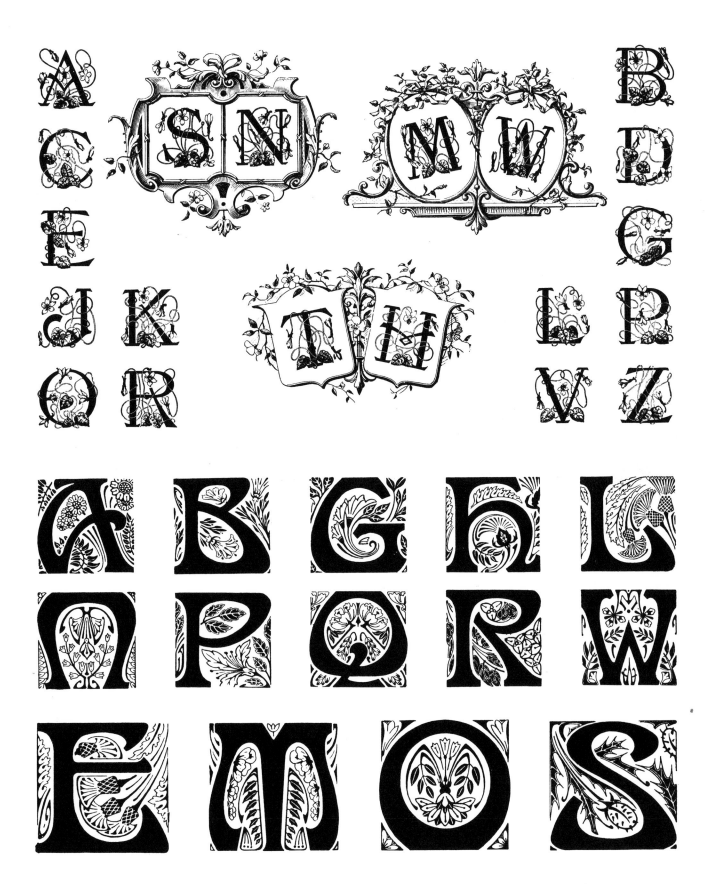

Sources for supplies

Ivory Nuts and Polishing Compound:
>Tumb-L-Matic Co.
>Box 132
>South Windsor, Connecticut 06074

There is no catalog available, but I talked to the owner who is quite friendly and will send you any information that you need. They have tumbling equipment, and if you are purchasing a large quantity, they will do your polishing for you.

>Donald R. Kostecki
>Lapidary Supplies
>6245 North Fairfield
>Chicago, Illinois 60659

He sells ivory nuts for $1.00 each; whalebone discs, flat, semi-polished, 40 mm for $2.00 each and 50 mm round at $2.50 each; and whale's teeth for Illinois residents until law changes.

Jewelry Findings:
Findings are all the parts of jewelry that are usually thought of as fasteners, such as clips and screws for earrings, pin backs, cuff link and tie tack attachments, fasteners for necklaces and bracelets, chains, and connectors.

>Ballou Findings
>810 Waterman Ave.
>East Providence, Rhode Island 02914

They carry all kinds of findings as well as catches and chains in gold, sterling silver, gold filled, and nickel silver.

>Metal City Findings Corp.
>450 West 31st St.
>New York, New York 10001

>S. Axelrod Co., Inc.
>9 West 30th St.
>New York, New York 10001

They carry key chains, neck chains, earring findings, footage chain, hooks, rings, and tassels.

New York Chain Mfg. Co. Inc.
32–20 38th Ave.
Long Island City, New York 11101

Novel Products Co.
42–61 24th St.
Long Island City, New York 11101

General Findings
7049½ Vineland Ave.
North Hollywood, California 91605

608 Fifth Ave.
New York, New York 10020

801 E. Marion St.
Arlington Heights
Chicago, Illinois 60004

Jeweler's Tools:
Allcraft Tool and Supply Co. Inc.
15 West 45th St.
New York, New York 10036
They have an extensive catalog and carry tools, findings, chain.

William Dixon Co.
752 Washington Avenue
Carlstadt, New Jersey 07072

Plastic Piano Keys:
Pratt, Read and Co.
Ivoryton, Connecticut 06442
If you write to them, you will receive a price list and instructions
for ordering. A set of fifty-two ivory colored, plastic keys comes
in a plastic package and costs approximately fifteen dollars.

Scrimshander's Tools:

    Scribing tools:
    X-Acto
    45-35 Van Dam Street
    Long Island City, New York 11101

    Motor tools and electric engraver:
    Dremel
    Department 864C
    Racine, Wisconsin 53406

Tripoli Polishing Compound (sometimes called gem polish):
This is a jeweler's polishing compound which is applied to the
surface of your work before beginning to do scrimshaw. Apply it
with a cloth or a piece of leather by hand, or it can be used with a
wheel rotated by a motor as Carol Arnold uses it.

    The Exolon Co.
    950 E. Niagra St.
    Tonawanda, New York 14150

    The George Basch Co., Inc.
    17 Hanse Avenue
    Freeport, New York 11520

Whalebone:
    P. J. McNally
    144 Chambers St.
    New York, New York 10007
He sells whale's teeth (can only be purchased by New York resi-
dents) whalebone, baleen, and scribers.

Bibliography

Ashley, Clifford. *The Yankee Whaler*. Boston: Houghton Mifflin, 1926.

Barnes, Clare, Jr. *John F. Kennedy, Scrimshaw Collector*, Boston: Little, Brown, 1969.

Benchley, Peter. "Life's Tempo On Nantucket." *National Geographic Society*, June 1970.

Burrows, Fredrika Alexander. *The Yankee Scrimshanders*. Taunton, Massachusetts: William S. Sullwold Pub., 1973.

Crosby, Everett U. *Susan's Teeth and Much about Scrimshaw*. Nantucket, Massachusetts: Tetaukimmo Press, 1955.

Cowley, Susan. "Whaling and Whalers, A Living Remembrance." *Americana, The American Heritage Society's Magazine*, January 1974.

Flayderman, Norman. *Scrimshaw and Scrimshanders*. New Milford, Connecticut: Flayderman, 1972.

Frere-Cook, Gervis. *The Decorative Arts of the Mariner*. Boston: Little, Brown and Company, 1966.

Gilkerson, William. *The Scrimshander*. San Francisco: Troubador Press, 1975.

Laing, Alexander. *Seafaring America*. New York: American Heritage Publishing Company, 1974.

Maskell, Alfred. *Ivories*. Rutland, Vermont: Charles E. Tuttle, 1966.

Plowden, David and Coffin, Patricia. *Nantucket*. New York: Viking Press, 1971.

Ritchie, Carson I. A. *Scrimshaw*. New York: Sterling Pub., 1972.

Stackpole, Edouard A. *Scrimshaw at Mystic Seaport*. Mystic, Connecticut: The Marine Historical Association, 1958.